UNCLASSIFIED: MY LIFE BEFORE, DURING, AND AFTER THE CIA

RICHARD JAMES KERR

Rand-Smith Publishing
Ashland

Unclassified: My Life Before, During, and After the CIA

Copyright ©2020 by Richard J. Kerr ALL RIGHTS RESERVED

The CIA Publication Board has approved the manuscript for publication.

No part of this book may be reproduced in any form or by any means (electronic, mechanical, digital, photocopy) without permission in writing from the publisher.

All photos from author's private collection unless otherwise indicated.

Print ISBN: 9781950544103

Digital ISBN: 9781950544110

Rand-Smith Publishing

Ashland, VA

www.Rand-Smith.com

Printed in the USA

Also by Richard J. Kerr:

The Dark Side of Paradise: Odd and Intriguing Stories from Vero Beach

CONTENTS

Dedication v

Introduction 1

PART I. IRAN AND PAKISTAN

1. Moving Misadventures 5
2. The Astute Recruit 12
3. Southern Discomfort 21
4. The Agency 25

PART II. LOS ANGELES

5. Briefing the President 61
6. Acting Director of Central Intelligence 106
7. Colleagues 112
8. Travel, Travel, Travel 127

9.	CIA Assessment	133
10.	Leaving CIA	144
11.	Russia and Beyond	156

PART III. BELFAST

12.	The "Irish Problem"	173
13.	Life on the Water	183

PART IV. VERO BEACH

14.	Digging Vero Beach	191
15.	Epilogue – Restoring the Importance of the Intelligence Community	195
16.	PHOTOS	198

DEDICATION

To my children and grandchildren.
May you have a happy life.

INTRODUCTION

After graduating from college, I serendipitously landed a job as a junior analyst at the Central Intelligence Agency. I was married and ready to begin my career, but I had no idea what was in store for me. Most of the people I met came from Ivy League schools or had been in the Office of Strategic Services. What began as an overwhelming and sometimes intimidating experience morphed into a thirty-year career where I was eventually tapped for the position of Acting Director.

During my time in the organization, I never worked for anyone substantively incompetent. The people I knew in the CIA were intelligent, focused, and committed. Some were better managers than others and some were task masters. I was never told to write or say something that I could not personally support. I delivered bad news to policymakers but was never told to soften my words. During my tenure, there were mundane, rote responsibilities, but also some historical, challenging events that I was honored to be a part of.

Life did not end when I left the CIA. I was asked to join a commission monitoring the Good Friday Agreement in Northern Ireland and then to assess the intelligence provided to policymakers before the Iraq war, among many other post-CIA adventures.

Throughout my professional journey, I met many important, powerful people and found myself in situations that I could never have imagined as a young college graduate with a new wife and a zeal to take on the world.

Being retired from the organization has given me the opportunity to reflect on my experiences. I hope that my stories provide a fresh, enlightening, "insider" perspective that helps others better understand the inner workings of that historic American institution. I can honestly say that I was proud to work at the CIA and always thought of it as more than just a "government job."

Then, and even now, when I'm asked if I worked for the government, I always say, "No, I worked for the CIA."

Finally, this memoir describes the day-to-day life of a CIA officer. It is the story of an ordinary person growing up in an incredibly complex organization who had some extraordinary experiences.

PART I

IRAN AND PAKISTAN

I was sitting in first class of an Air France passenger jet on my way to Tehran where I would change planes for my arrival in Karachi, Pakistan. The purpose was to brief the Shah of Iran and the President of Pakistan on the Soviet strategic threat. I was alone except for a security officer carrying a large case containing satellite imagery of Russian missile sites, submarine shipyards, and other military equipment. I was 29 years old, married with three children, and on my sixth year of working for the Central Intelligence Agency. I was still a junior analyst and although it was my first trip abroad, it was not my first briefing of senior officials. It still amazed me that I was now working for the CIA.

The path getting to this point in my life was that of a gypsy. I need to explain.

1.

MOVING MISADVENTURES

Divorce was not unusual in my family. My grandfather and grandmother apparently had a huge argument after being married long enough to have seven children. My grandmother drove a horse and wagon from their farm to nearby Oregon City, OR, leaving my grandfather and the children to fend for themselves. After some time in Oregon City, my grandmother said she wanted to return to the family. My grandfather, a stubborn Scotsman, refused to let her come back.

I do not know the circumstances leading to my parents' divorce when I was two years old. I went with my mother, and my older brother went with my father. I do know that they seldom talked to each other again unless it was about where I was to be sent.

Then my mother met my stepfather, Charles Heddy, in Seaside, Oregon, and that began my adventure in travel. Between 1938 and 1950, I lived in about 25 different towns and went to more than 20 different schools in four states. When I filled out my application for employment with the

CIA, they asked for the address in each town I had lived in, the schools I attended, and the name of each teacher. I did as well as I could, but in some cases I could not even sort out the right town in the right year.

From what I understood, all our moving was because my stepfather could not get a job he wanted and could not keep a job he could get. One of my cousins, who knew my mother and stepfather when they were first married, told me years later that he was a "nogoodnik." I'm not sure how accurate that assessment is, but on the other hand, all things considered, even at a young age I could tell they loved each other. So, we continued to move, and I felt like a set of China that the wife insists come along, despite her husband's grumbling.

This is what I listed on my CIA entrance papers, which I am sure was an anomaly to them, especially in those days:

1935 — Fort Smith, Arkansas
1935 — Portland, Oregon (Aunt Hazel's)
1937 — Seaside, Oregon
1938 — Portland, Oregon (Lived with my stepfather's Aunt Meta)
1939 — Oakland, California
1939 — Portland, Oregon (Aunt Hazel's)
1939 — Gerhart, Oregon
1940 — Seaside, Oregon
1941 — Portland, Oregon (Aunt Hazel's)
1941 — Pacific Palisades, California
1942 — Twin Falls, Idaho
1942 — Ilwaco, Washington
1943 — Topanga Canyon, California
1943 — McLoughlin Heights, Vancouver, California
1944 — Kitty Hawk, California

1945 — Portland, Oregon (Aunt Hazel's)
1945 — Red Bluff, California
1946 — Dunsmuir, California
1946 — Cannon Beach, Oregon
1946 — Reedsport, Oregon
1948 — San Luis Obispo, California
1948 — Morro Bay, California
1949 — Cupertino, California

It's no surprise that moving played havoc with schooling and not just on an academic level. It was impossible to make close friends when attending a school for a few months at best. Because of my circumstances, I learned things other than English, arithmetic, science, and whatever else was taught in grade school. I learned how to survive as the new kid in class. I learned how to be invisible, and how to run fast to escape bullies. I learned how to be independent. There was little choice.

The Golden Gate International Exposition (GGIE) was a World's Fair held in San Francisco in 1939 to celebrate the recently constructed San Francisco-Oakland Bay Bridge (1936) and the Golden Gate Bridge (1937). The event took place on Treasure Island, a man-made island funded by the federal government as an airport before the idea was nixed. So, that site in the San Francisco Bay was used for the GGIE.

I was only four or five at the time, but I remember being captivated by the hypnotic blinking lights of the huge Ferris wheel that rose high above the other rides and exhibits. My parents worked at the fair, as did many in the area. One of my cousins told me years later that she came down to San Francisco and took me back to Portland by train to reunite with my biological father. I don't know why I was sent away, possibly because they would be consumed by their jobs at the fair which ran from February 18 to October 29, 1939 and then again from May 25 to September 29, 1940. Regardless of the circumstances, I returned to live with my mother fairly soon thereafter.

When we moved to California at the beginning of WWII, we rented a house that was part of a large estate in Pacific Palisades. The house had been the home of the family's driver. It looked directly down on the Pacific Ocean and from the window I could see my mother, who became a warden, walking along the beach with her book filled with the silhouettes of Japanese fighter aircraft.

During the early years of WWII, both my mother and stepfather worked at the shipyard in Long Beach. They worked the night shift so that meant I was alone. One night I went to see the movie *The Wolf Man* starring Lon Chaney. It so frightened me that I spent the rest of the night sitting on a neighbor's porch. I have been afraid of werewolves ever since.

Always searching for something better, my stepfather read an ad for an onsite handyman to perform repairs at a farm in Dunsmuir, California. Dunsmuir is on a wild part of the Sacramento River in the northern part of the state, and the farm was several miles outside of town. My stepfather, Chuck, fancied himself many things, but a handyman he was not. His new job was a disaster, and the only thing that kept us from starving was an apple orchard. I helped my mother pick apples and she made whatever she could think of—apple pie, turnovers, boiled apples baked apples, fried apples, apple sauce. I could not eat apples for years after that. I'd had my fill.

As is typical on farms, there were several feral cats and they drove Chuck crazy. One day, he managed to round them all up in a gunnysack that he promptly threw into the river. He was a desperate type of guy, so his actions didn't surprise me, but I was upset for those kittens. The next day, by some miracle, the pesky felines returned to continue wreaking havoc on Chuck and the farm.

In 1942, Chuck got a job surveying the layout of the Minidoka Japanese internment camp being constructed just outside of Twin Falls, Idaho. I am not sure how my parents got to Twin Falls, but I was taken to Los Angeles and placed on a train, under the care of a conductor, to make the journey by myself.

Just after the war, our family ended up in Red Bluff, California. We stayed with one of my mother's friends for well over a month and finally drove off in a beat-up pickup with all our belongings in the back and me sitting in an overstuffed chair. As we continued the long climb on the highway north, the back wheel of the pickup came off and the left side of the truck slammed to the ground with a jarring crash, forcing us to return to Red Bluff.

Once again, I was sent off to my father's house in Reedsport, Oregon, where he lived with a fairly new wife and my older brother. It was an excruciatingly long trip on a Greyhound bus, and I spent several months there. I found out years later that my stepmother had not been told that my father had more than one son until I showed up.

One summer we were going north and did not have enough money for gas so every day or so we stopped at orchards and picked fruit. Once we even harvested hops.

It was always a fun diversion for me, but I don't think my parents were particularly amused.

Sometime in the early 1940s, my mother was diagnosed with breast cancer. I was never aware of what was going on because I was again sent off to my father's, this time so she could undergo a mastectomy. I found out later the seriousness of the operation, but there was never any discussion with me about the cancer or her condition. That was a time when people kept things to themselves and pushed on.

At one point, things were finally going well. By sheer persistence, Chuck and my mother had found jobs that seemed to suit them. He had a maintenance position at a local college, and she started a business selling Stanley Home Products door to door. She held parties at people's homes and sang the praises of various cleaning tools and household products. Apparently, she had an aptitude for the work and made enough money to buy a new Chevy sedan.

Being in one spot was a luxury for me and allowed me to become well-established in school, actually making good friends like Phil Tuson, and even having a girlfriend, Carol Arnold, even if she didn't know it.

My dog, Vicki, was a constant companion as we wandered the open countryside near our home, which had become a project itself. Because my parents thought they had found a place they wanted to say, they had decided to build a house. While it was under construction, my parents lived in a large tent that included a kitchen, dining table, and their bedroom. My younger brother, Steve, lived in the tent with them. I was relegated to a much smaller tent next door. Still, I didn't mind because we were in one location. My dog and I had our own "home," and it was great.

One evening I heard my mother crying, and I stood outside their tent listening to the conversation. She was sobbing uncontrollably. The doctor had told her that the cancer had come back and she would not live long. I heard her say, "What is going to happen to my babies?"

I came home from school one day and found we were moving yet again. My dog had been given away, the house we had built was sold, and everything was packed up. We moved first to a motel in Morro Bay and then to live with my stepfather's brother in Cupertino, California. As usual, no one bothered to tell me what was going or why we had moved.

In September of 1950, my mother died at the age of thirty-nine. I moved to Roseburg, Oregon, to live with my father and stepmother. My travelling days were largely over.

While I had many adventures during our vagabond lifestyle, I longed to stay in one place for more than a few months. I wanted to make friends and feel like I belonged somewhere. It reached the point where I'd attend a new school and not even attempt to get settled. I knew that at any time I could come home to find that we were moving again. It had not been an unhappy life to that point. I had been treated well, had some adventures, and learned a bit about life.

But even then, I decided that if and when I became a father, things would be different for my own family.

2.

THE ASTUTE RECRUIT

I was a social misfit, and my "new" family and my home life was not good therapy. In my father's household, they led an insulated lifestyle, and that did not change with my presence. My father made a good living as a logging consultant, and they lived in a nice house in a middle-class neighborhood. Over the next three years with my father, stepmother, and half-sister, we never once went out to dinner, never had guests at the house, and only one or two visits from relatives. We never went on vacation or took trips to the ocean or anywhere else. It was completely different from my former life where we were practically gypsies meeting people everywhere that we went.

    I realize in hindsight that what I needed was a warm, welcoming family that would widen my life experiences and teach me what life was all about, but that was not to be. My father and stepmother had strong values, few if any prejudices, and were good role models for the most part. My attitude and tendency to keep to myself certainly did not help, but it was difficult for me to switch gears after so many years living a totally different way.

Initially, I rebelled. I plotted my escape from the family. Reading in my room and meeting up with school friends became the focal point of my life. I had spent a month in Roseburg the summer before my mother died, and I had met a couple of local boys at the swimming pool. Luckily, they were very popular and knew everyone in town. When I started high school, my two friends made sure I was a part of the group.

Life in Roseburg in the early 1950s was good—a small town supported by the timber industry with traditional "western values" and some of the populist views of traditional Oregon. The school was very welcoming, and I seemed to fit in well. It was surprisingly free of class distinctions and prejudice, although there were the natural cliques and groupings of friends. I decided to put my escape plans on hold.

As an educational experience, Roseburg High School was a disaster, at least for me. I came to high school totally unprepared in the basics thanks to my unstructured academic history. However, I was able to learn some leadership skills, and I was even elected Senior Class President. I must admit I spent far too much time leading friends in amusing, unconstructive hi-jinks.

I was in a journalism class that had an advisor but no regular teacher because it was primarily involved in producing the school newspaper. One day, I suggested that we skip school and go to the high schools of nearby towns, saying we were visiting various schools in the area to learn about their journalism classes and their newspapers. Off we went. We were given the royal treatment at the first school, placed in a conference room as students were taken out of class to talk with us. It was all very professional and very ad hoc. Our visit was so successful that we did not make it to a second school. We hadn't expected to get as far as we had.

My English teacher, Mr. Ewing, was a bit controversial. I had always been a voracious reader and dove into anything I could get my hands on. Mr. Ewing got me started writing essays and reading 19th-century Russian novels. This was during the 1950s when there was a lot of talk about blacklists and traitors. During my junior year, he was accused by someone in the community of being a communist, and there was talk he would be fired. In protest and a show of solidarity, the students organized a strike and a parade in downtown Roseburg. Everyone walked out of class. It was very empowering, and Mr. Ewing stayed on as a teacher.

Mr. Hoffman was a tennis coach who regularly sent players to the State finals, and when I was on the team, I was a bit intimidated because they were proud of winning 73 matches without a loss. I just made the team—fifth man—but never lost a match and continued to play tennis for decades. Being part of a successful team helped me build confidence, athleticism, and a sense of belonging.

A few months into the academic year, I was in the audience at a school event. On the stage I saw a short, attractive red head with a very good figure. I had to get to know that girl! I found out her name was Janice Sinclair, and that she had moved to Roseburg to live with her mother before the ninth grade.

Jan and I began to date our senior year and after graduation, we decided to get married. However, there was an issue. I was seventeen and my father would not give me permission to marry. I had no money for college and was not prepared in any case. I did not want to work in some local job and be stuck in Roseburg. I had wanderlust, and I wanted to get out of that town.

Jan and I decided that I should join the army and then go to college on the GI bill as a way to get our life started. We would get married after I finished 16 weeks of basic training—I would then be 18—and go wherever the army sent us. We felt like we had made a very mature and grownup decision. My father was happy to provide consent for that.

The Army
On June 23, 1953, I joined the army at a recruiting office in Roseburg Oregon. A few days later, I took a bus to Fort Lewis in Washington state, a large reception center during the Korean War. After three days of processing and three days on kitchen patrol (KP) from 0600 to 2400, I decided that I did not like the army all that much. But it was too late! I had made a decision, and I had to learn what it meant to honor that. I was sent to Ford Ord, California, for 16 weeks of basic training as a grunt in the infantry.

I was assigned to a company that was quartered in tents far away from the more permanent part of the post. The company was made up of a few "innocents" from the West Coast—most just out of high school but a few draftees, one with a law degree and another with a doctorate in psychology. The bulk of the company of more than 200 men was drawn from large cities throughout the middle of the US. They were a bit older and were primarily troublemakers or "criminals" who were given the choice by a judge of joining the army or being sentenced to jail. Few were hardened criminals, but most had been involved in car theft, robberies, habitual shoplifting or other minor crimes. They were a tough group accustomed to fighting and standing up to authority.

The army had its own troublemakers recently returned or sent back from Korea—officers and non-commissioned officers—who had been disciplined and, in some cases, demoted but not kicked out of the service. What better example to set for my company? Clearly the intention was to keep us in line. It was the *Dirty Dozen* film without the movie stars.

Because of our crew of misfits, we were treated much differently than the other companies. We ran to all our training areas, some miles away from our camp. We carried M-1 rifles, and wore packs and steel helmets. The officers and NCOs carried nothing and wore caps. After a couple of weeks of running, the younger soldiers were in pretty good shape and we would run up behind the NCO leading us and someone would ask, "Could we could speed it up a bit? We are getting sleepy." Then the jibes would begin. "Sarge, you are getting a bit old for this. How old are you, 35 or 40? This running can't be good for someone your age and someone with a big gut. A heart attack is a real possibility."

Once we were on a firing range where each company crawled under barbed wire while machine guns fired live rounds over their heads. When it came to our turn, the entire company went out under the wire and would not come out. We just lay there and rested for more than an hour while the officers and NCO ranted over the loudspeakers at the end of the range. Finally, they stopped firing and turned on all the lights and we ran back to camp, only to be told later to fall out of the tents for a full inspection. Also, our company did not get the opportunity to throw live grenades. I think our NCOs and officers were afraid to get into a trench with us and grenades.

We went out for exercise in a nearby area. A few of us were standing around and told by an NCO to wait right there. We did. We waited and waited. When it was time for chow, we went over to the area where everyone ate and then returned to our spot. Every so often, an NCO or officer would come by and shout, "What the hell are you guys doing?" We would respond by saying we were told to stay right where we were. Three days later, we went back to our camp having never left the area.

My company was never very good at games except for boxing and the struggle pit. We had a lot of people who had been in street fights, so they had been training for the sport most of their lives. In boxing, opponents were put up against a person of similar height. I was 6 foot 3 and weighed 150 pounds. I was matched against a fellow who was 6 foot 4 and weighed about 250, all muscle. I danced around and tried not to hit him, and he just played with me, landing a punch now and then, but making sure he did not hurt me. The referee finally called off the match as a waste of time. In the struggle pit, the last person remaining in the sand was the winner. We always won.

Despite our ability to excel in a couple of events, or possibly because of it, we were always treated differently than the others, and to top it off, we got no weekend leave for 16 weeks. We were harassed and hassled, cursed and physically abused. The interesting thing was that the more difficult the treatment, the more challenging it became and the closer the company came together. Maybe that was the plan all along. I'm not sure how I got lumped in with that group of misfits, but I learned much more than I had ever anticipated.

Because of their brushes with the law, those guys knew how to beat the system. I was not as street smart, so I decided that the secret was to keep my head down and avoid direct confrontation while still paying attention and looking for opportunities. To my surprise, we all became loyal to one another, helped the weaker and innocent, and became a solid group of recruits and all-around good guys.

Getting Married

After basic training, I returned to Roseburg. I was now 18 and did not need permission to marry, and as planned, Jan and I made the arrangements. Neither my parents nor Jan's father and new stepmother came to the wedding. I am not even sure they were invited, but it was nice that Jan's mother attended.

I wasn't able to get too comfortable because shortly after we were married, I was stationed at Ft. Sheridan near Chicago. It was a military installation that received soldiers from Korea who were getting out of the army. Lots of people came through there and it seemed very disorganized. As I was putting my gear on my bunk, a soldier asked if I minded if he settled next to me. "Fine by me," I said, "unless you have some strange habits." He said, "No, I don't think so, but I am Jewish." I had never met anyone who was Jewish and didn't know how to respond, so I just nodded.

Someone was always looking for strays to put on KP or other duties. Learning from my time with the Dirty Dozen, several of us found an NCO with a clipboard to march us around the post keeping us out of assignments and usually close to a chow line. I didn't have to worry too much because in no time, I was shipped out.

My next assignment was Camp Carson (later Fort Carson) located in Colorado Springs, Colorado. I was assigned to a headquarters company and on the second day we were in a formation next to a bunch of tanks—the 11th Calvary was getting ready to go to Korea. The NCO in charge asked if there was anyone who could type. I had learned from the Dirty Dozen never to raise my hand and volunteer for anything, but tanks and Korea changed my mind. I was assigned to Division Headquarters where I spent the next year as a file clerk.

On the positive side, it did not take long for me to find out how to get Jan to Camp Carson. I rented a one-room-plus apartment in Colorado Springs and Jan took the train from Roseburg. We were living good on $120 per month. Jan found a job first at a drug store soda fountain and then at a private school. We were living an austere but good life, with no car, no money, no cares, and lots of love. What more did we need?

While at Fort Carson, I went to a dentist to have wisdom teeth pulled, and the headquarters company I was assigned to listed me as being in the hospital. For several months I regularly checked the duty rosters each morning before I reported to my job at division headquarters. I was never on a list for guard duty or KP, or more importantly for shipment to Korea. There were a number of levies for Korea during those months and my name never came up. My basic training experience told me to never ask why you are not on a duty list. At one point I saw my name with a note saying, "Report to the company clerk." When I showed up, he said, "Glad to see you are out of the hospital." A bit puzzled, I kept my mouth shut.

A year after getting to Camp Carson, I found I had orders to report to Ft. Monroe in Virginia for assignment as a clerk typist for the planning staff of a very large military exercise. By that time, Jan and I had purchased our first car and we decided to drive east ourselves. For the next year, I planned, or typed plans, for the largest military exercise held in the US (Exercise Sagebrush)that took over most of the state of Louisiana, operating out of Camp Polk.

Things seemed to be working out in spite of my unconventional upbringing, but I still had a lot to learn.

3.

SOUTHERN DISCOMFORT

Living in Virginia, in the heart of the confederacy, my wife and I had our first immersive experiences with other races. In Roseburg at that time, diversity just did not exist. In the army, I had begun to learn more about other people like my Jewish bunk mate and African Americans who were part of the Dirty Dozen, but that was a controlled environment.

When we moved to the Norfolk area, we found a small shotgun-style house with cheap rent and took it. One interesting thing about that little house, which was about 8 feet wide with rooms laid out in a straight line. Someone had fired a bullet through a window that went the length of house, through several walls, and came out a window at the other end. That was taking the style of house literally, and it was concerning.

We did not realize for some time that the residents in the area were predominantly minorities. It just wasn't something that even occurred to us. Everyone was welcoming and we assimilated effortlessly, walking around the community, shopping at the grocery stores, eating at soul food restaurants, but soon it became clear that we were in the segregated South. It became obvious that we didn't understand the complex history involved. We just liked the area.

At Camp Polk, I became friends with an NCO who was African American. I asked him one evening if he wanted to go into town and get a beer. He looked at me as if I was crazy. "Do you know what would happen if the two of us showed up in town? This is the deep South and blacks and whites do not drink in the same bars without consequences." In the month we spent at Camp Polk, he never once left the post.

We settled into family life in Virginia and on September 20, 1955, our son Randall Alan Kerr was born. A few days later, I left for Camp Polk leaving Jan alone for more than a month in a new apartment with a new baby. It was not the last time I was called away, leaving her with the responsibility for children, the house, bills, and everything else.

Off to College

I was able to finish up my three years in the army in Colorado Springs. Then, according to plan, I attended the University of Oregon on the GI bill to get an education and provide a good life for my growing family. I registered for classes with a friend from high school who had just gotten out of the Air Force. He had been a bright but difficult student at Roseburg High. As we were talking outside of the Student Union one day, we were amazed to see our high school principal walk by. He stopped and asked with real surprise, "What are the two of you doing here?" We responded that we were starting school. Without hesitation he said, "You will never make it."

We *did* make it. My friend went on to get a doctorate and ended up as the department head of the history department of a small Midwestern college. My time at the University of Oregon went by nearly as fast as my army stint—three years as an undergraduate and one year in graduate school. In my third year, I was a grader for a history class and a teaching assistant the following year.

My thesis advisor got me involved in a project well beyond my capabilities—the history of the first Russian Duma, the Tsarist attempt at representative government. The problem was he wanted me to use primary sources and my Russian was not good enough to do serious research. I tried and spent the summer of 1960 at the Hoover Institute working in their vast library. It was a struggle and to top it off, I really did not know how to organize a research project. I also had a family to support. I desperately needed a paying job.

We lived in veteran housing for $34 a month. I worked several jobs at the same time—school bus driver (morning and afternoon), service station in the afternoons, bakery and cleaning cars on the weekends. I took very heavy class loads, usually more than 20 hours. I studied hard because my family was growing. Andre was born on December 31, 1958, and Kevin in September of 1960. Having been in the army and already married with children, I didn't have the typical college experience. I don't think I attended a single sporting event in my four years. I was consumed with classes, studying, working, and trying to spend time with my family.

My plan had been to get a master's degree and then

a teaching job at some small college while continuing to work on a doctorate. But my guardian angel was watching over me, and I attended a session where a representative from the Central Intelligence Agency was recruiting graduates.

I went for an interview and put in an application.

4.

THE AGENCY

1960
US President: Dwight D. Eisenhower
CIA Director: Allen Dulles

A few months after my application, the CIA sent a letter asking me to come to Washington DC for testing, background interviews, and more. I couldn't believe my good fortune. For the first time in my twenty-five years, I boarded an airplane and flew to the nation's capital. I was put up in a small hotel in Georgetown and given an address to report to at 0900.

When I got to the address the next day, I was disappointed to see a nondescript townhouse, not the ornate architecture I had imagined. However, I didn't have time to worry about that as I was quickly ushered into a room to begin the testing process, more interviews, more background forms to complete, and finally a polygraph. Back then, being required to take one was quite rare, and understandably, many thoughts ran through my head. Should I tell them that I had taken money out of my mother's purse to buy some candy when I was a child? What should I expect? Was it ok to be nervous? The test administrators were there to ask questions, not give answers, so I knew I was on my own. I embraced the process and decided to trust my instincts. I was confident in the fact that I did not have a long list of sins and certainly no conversations with Russian spies.

I returned to Oregon and waited for some indication that I was going to be hired. I was anxious and eager to get some news after such an immersive interview process. Also, I knew that I needed to secure a good job to support my family. Then it happened. At the end of the summer, I received a letter offering me a position as an analyst. The yearly salary was $5,300 and the position was the lowest analyst level, GS-7. (Analysts at CIA could reach GS-14. Before I left CIA, I had moved to the EP-4 the level of Deputy cabinet officers, 15 grades higher than where I started). I was not told what I would be working, but I had to relocate to Washington DC by the reporting date. I didn't even think to ask if they would pay my travel expenses (they would have).

The idea of working for a secret organization in Washington was exciting. The fact that they would pay me that extravagant salary was frosting on the cake. I quickly accepted the CIA offer thinking that a couple of years would be interesting and if it did not work out, I could always go back to Oregon and get a teaching job.

The trip east was not without drama. We bought a Ford station wagon for the journey and rented a small trailer. We crammed all of our belongings into the car and trailer including bed springs filled with cans of vegetables given to us by Jan's parents. On top of the springs was a mattress, which meant the three boys had about two feet of head space for the entire ride. Then we found out the two oldest boys had the mumps during the trip. Our youngest boy was only a month old, and fortunately, he seemed healthy. Then a tire blew out on a bridge crossing the Mississippi. We did not have sufficient funds to stay in motels every night, so we often slept in the car. It was a difficult trip, but we were young, eager, and determined.

Eventually, we arrived in Alexandria, Virginia, and after stopping at a real estate office, were told that they in fact had a house for rent. The only problem was that the renters had left in the night without paying or cleaning the house. It was a real mess, but if we were willing to clean it up, the first month was free. That was an amazing deal for a cash-poor couple, so we eagerly accepted.

I started working for the agency just after the CIA's U-2 spy plane piloted by Francis Gary Powers was shot down over Russia and four months before the abortive "Bay of Pigs" invasion of Cuba.

Processing in was easy because most of the paperwork had been completed during my earlier trip to DC. After a couple of days, I was told to report to an office called the Industrial Register. If I had known what my job there was going to involve, I might have just packed up the car and headed back west.

I first worked in a building that had been a skating rink; there was still a sign high on the wall that read, "All Skate." It was a huge facility with small work compartments holding several desks. As it turned out, I worked in an old vault where I was reading and filing reports about German POWs returning from Russia. Most had been working in Russian factories moved from

Germany at the end of the war. The job was boring, and any real contribution to understanding the Soviet economy was minuscule. It was not long before I began to reconsider my professional choices.

Then the CIA moved into its new building in Langley, Virginia. I still held the same job, but my work area was in the building with the rest of the Agency. I felt much more connected and involved just being around everyone. I'd learned from my army experience that if you want something, it's up to you to take the initiative. So, I decided to walk the halls of the new facility and take note of the various departments, hoping one might spark my interest. I saw a sign for the Office of Basic Intelligence (OBI), went in, and asked to see the Director. A somewhat hesitant secretary called the boss and said someone wanted to talk with him about a job.

I met a man named Bruce Clarke, and I told him about my interest in finding a job that better suited my interests. I stressed that I wasn't picky. In fact, I was willing to do almost anything that felt like a challenge. We had a long conversation about my background and education, and I'm sure he had seen many eager new hires champing at the bit to become immersed in the Agency. Fortunately, he was willing to give me a chance. He had a vacancy for an analyst doing work about Thailand! That wasn't exactly what I'd imagined, but I jumped at the opportunity. Bruce and I forged a great relationship, and he became my boss and an influential mentor for the next 20 years.

My first assignment in OBI was to write a comprehensive report on the structure and functioning of the Thai government. It was a challenge to organize the project, find source material, and go through what turned out to be a major editorial review, but I was eager and went at it with enthusiasm.

Like many young married couples, it was not long before we bought our first home, a semi-detached house in Alexandria. It was a good location for our family, close to a grade school and in an area filled with young families and many children. We did all the typical family things—got a dog, signed the oldest boy up for little league baseball, and began soaking up the local history with weekend trips to forts, museums, and all the sights. I was determined to remain steadfast to my pledge to give my children a different upbringing than I'd had.

1962
US President: John F. Kennedy
CIA Director: John A. McCone

In 1962, I reported to work one day to find that the Office of Basic Intelligence was being abolished. Its personnel were scattered, and most went to the Office of Current Intelligence. I was told that I would be assigned to the group responsible for the Far East, but the Cuban Missile Crisis had begun with the discovery of strategic missile sites under construction on the island. That meant additional bodies were needed to staff the CIA 24-hour Operations Center, so I was sent there as a watch officer.

The Russians had been shipping military equipment to Cuba for some time. I had been blissfully unaware of developments there as I focused on Thailand. The Russians had deployed a SA-2 surface-to-missile system around Cuba, provided coastal defense missiles, and sent in medium range bombers. Three armored divisions were sent in clandestinely. Then U-2 photography showed medium and intermediate range missile sites under construction. At that point, the US imposed a blockade with the US Navy turning back Soviet supply ships. The US President demanded that the missile, and Soviet units, be withdrawn.

The CIA was often criticized for not having anticipated the deployment of Soviet strategic missile to Cuba. The military buildup on the Island had been monitored and reported, but the idea that the Russians would directly challenge the US by deploying nuclear weapons in Cuba seemed a bit of a reach. Also, it was important to remember that the missiles were detected and monitored by U-2 aircraft and satellites developed by the CIA. In hindsight, the Soviet leadership seemed to believe that there was little difference between deploying missiles to Cuba and the US setting up missile sites in Turkey. They miscalculated. Nuclear-tipped missiles 100 miles off the US coast were not something the US would tolerate.

On October 27, I was in the Operations Center when a SA-2 missile shot down a U-2 aircraft on a reconnaissance mission over Cuba. Some senior US military officials wanted to respond with a major strike against all the SA-2 sites in Cuba. But cooler heads prevailed, and the Russians and US agreed to several conditions for ending the crisis; the US would withdraw missile units from Turkey and promised not to invade Cuba, and the Russians would withdraw all strategic weapons and ground forces from the island.

As CIA Director, John McCone was impressive. Out of the private sector, his shipyards had built "Liberty" ships during WWII. He was wealthy, independent, and confident. He also focused attention on what was happening in Cuba. He had been concerned about the Soviet activity in Cuba for some time and was not all that surprised by Soviet actions.

McCone expected to be immediately informed about anything that happened on the island and even removed a senior duty officer for not getting some information to him during his dinner at the State Department. As the head of US intelligence, he was angry that he had to be informed about some development in Cuba by his host and not one of his officers.

I accompanied Director McCone on several congressional briefings as a bag carrier. Late one evening, as discussions ended about the next day's briefing on the Hill, the Director turned to me, reached into his pocket, and pulled out a money clip. My God, I thought, he is going to give me a tip. But he just turned away and walked out of the room.

McCone may be best remembered as being prescient about the Russian strategic buildup in Cuba, but from a CIA perspective, he should be immortalized as the person who transformed the CIA into a leading scientific and technical innovative organization. He hired Dr. Albert "Bud" Wheelon to head CIA's Office of Scientific Intelligence. Bud Wheelon soon became the head of a Directorate that included all of CIA's varied scientific and technical organizations. He led the development of photographic and electronic collection satellites and a host of other technical collection capabilities. He also attracted many highly qualified engineers and scientists to CIA making it the innovative leader in the Intelligence Community.

After several weeks in the Operations Center, I found

that Bruce Clarke had intervened and ended my assignment at the Far East Office. Instead, I was moved to the newly formed Cuban Branch in his new office. For a while, I was the only analyst in the unit. My immediate boss was John Hick, a larger-than-life person who became another mentor and close friend.

John was with the marines during the campaigns in the Pacific islands. He went on to become the Associate Deputy Director of Intelligence and the Director of the National Photographic Intelligence Center. John, two of his cronies, and I were regulars in croquet matches, and we became close family friends.

The Cuban Branch was responsible for current intelligence reporting on Soviet and Cuban military activity on the island. Obviously, there were many other units in the Agency following this issue, but our job was to perform the daily reporting on events, writing assessments on all aspects of the Cuban and Soviet military activity on the island, and give briefings inside the Agency, to Congress, and many others. Very quickly, our principle problem was to monitor the withdrawal of Soviet strategic weapons and military units. Another key question was which weapons were being transferred to the Cuban military.

New analysts were sent to the unit to handle the workload because the pressure to produce intelligence on Soviet and Cuban military activity was intense. There was a good deal of competition among the group. If someone came in at night to write a report on a breaking story, the other analysts would critique his work and suggest how it could have been improved. It was done with good humor, but the process also made everyone pay close attention to their analyses and what and how they wrote.

At one point, the Russians had agreed to withdraw their armored divisions. Were they doing what they promised? Some US fighters flew low-level photographic missions over the ground forces sites in Cuba. The photography went to the National Photographic Intelligence Center (NPIC), and a fellow analyst and I were sent down to the Center to determine if there were indications the Soviets were leaving. We spent the night with photo interpreters and wrote a memorandum that we had on the desk of the Director of Current Intelligence at 0700. It concluded that the Soviets were in fact pulling out their ground forces. This judgment was based on some fairly fragmentary evidence, but it was enough to give us confidence in our judgment. The Director of Current Intelligence called us to his office and asked how confident we were because he was about to send our report to the President. Putting on a good face, we said we would stand behind our judgment.

The Office of Current Intelligence was the premier organization in the analytic directorate. It was organized into regional divisions with the exception of Military Division. The office produced current intelligence, publishing a National Intelligence Daily publication and the President's Daily Brief among other publications.

The Military Division covered the world's militaries but focused on the USSR, China, and the Middle East. It had an interesting mix of older analysts of WWII vintage and young analysts brought in during CIA's burst of growth in the early 1960s. It had some remarkable people—one of the analysts was a small gray-haired lady who had parachuted into France with the OSS during WWII. There was also a retired Air Force Colonel who had piloted a bomber during the war. Most of the young analysts held graduated degrees but had little practical experience. Still, they were eager and competent, just the right combination.

I spent more than a year working in the Cuban Branch, a year filled with heavy pressure to produce daily intelligence on Cuba and the withdrawal of Soviets strategic forces from Cuba. The pressure of writing articles each day and many nights provided an important foundation for future assignments. Writing all types of products, and briefing senior Agency, US and foreign officials all under significant pressure to get it done quickly and right provided opportunities many analysts never experienced.

The year and a half that I spent working on the Soviet forces in Cuba was the foundation for future jobs in the Agency. I learned how to write and write quickly. Bruce Clarke and John Hicks, along with editors in the Office of Current Intelligence, reviewed everything that was produced. They demanded clear, unambiguous language with a strong topic sentence and a concise conclusion. The editing was unrelenting, and the only choices were to learn or fall by the wayside.

My experiences working on the Cuban missile crisis was a dramatic point in my career. I learned a great deal about the intelligence process and the excitement of being involved in events that had an impact on US foreign policy. I was thrown into the process of briefing senior officials and defending my analysis. I was given a good deal of independence although both Clarke and Hicks looked over my shoulder. I was learning and at the same time given encouragement. It did not take long for me to believe that I had found an organization that I believed would reward me for hard work and initiative. I believed that CIA was by far the most interesting organization in Washington and was critical to protecting the country. I never looked back; I was hooked. I was learning the business of intelligence and the excitement of being involved in the critical issue facing the US.

At home, Jan was put under a good deal of pressure during my Cuban drama. I worked long hours, weekends and nights. She managed the family and all that involved with three active boys. She worried that if Washington DC were attacked by the Russians, we were living too far southeast of the city to make our escape west. She was concerned by the news and local chatter, which is naturally intensified around the nation's capital. She had decided that moving west of DC would better our chances of getting out of the area in the event of an emergency. I understood her concern and agreed that if she would be more comfortable, by all means we should relocate.

The five of us began weekend trips on the western side of the CIA headquarters in Northern Virginia. Up and down Georgetown Pike, we often ended up in a small crossroad town called Great Falls. Our choices were limited by salary and the requirement for ten percent down for a home purchase. One Saturday we saw a small sign for a real estate agent, and we drove down a pipe stem road. We knocked on the door and told Mr. Peters we were looking for a house in the area. Without much hesitation, he said he was thinking about selling his own home. The house had three bedrooms and was made of cement block with a small garage, sitting on more than an acre of land.

It was an ideal starter house. He told us the price and we accepted, putting our attached home in Alexandria up for sale. It was a great opportunity for us, and there were great possibilities for expansion. It was also located near a grade school.

1964

US President: Lyndon B. Johnson
CIA Director: William Raborn / Richard Helms

After leaving the Cuban Branch, I spent the next six years working on the Soviet military. First, following Soviet strategic missile deployment inside Russia. After the Cuban missile crisis, the Soviets began deploying intercontinental missiles at a fast rate. New missile sites were scattered along the Trans-Siberian rail line from Moscow to the Far East. The US detected these new sites using an extraordinary satellite photographic program that blanketed the Soviet Union. A total of 18 new ICBM complexes were identified over the next few years. Keeping track of new sites and reporting on the various missile programs was a full-time job that occupied the time of many CIA and Defense Department analysts. Missile test ranges, test firings, storage facilities and nuclear weapons programs, and all the things necessary to develop, support, and operate the missile program came into play. My task was current intelligence reporting on these programs relying on the knowledge of photo interpreters and a vast array of other experts. It is worthwhile to point out that as I was learning to report current developments, I relied on a very impressive set of experts who had followed Soviet the military for years. I was just the penman living off their expertise. I do not believe that such a comprehensive collection effort and work force of more experts has ever been put together working on a single subject.

In March of 1966, Jan gave birth to a girl—a girl! Meagan Antoinette Kerr was an exciting addition to family. Although our oldest, Randy, said he was not sure we needed another family member when he heard that his mother was expecting, the three boys were always very protective of their baby sister.

The saying around the Agency was that if you didn't like your current position, just wait six months. Sure enough, it was not long before I got another assignment, the job of current intelligence analyst following the Soviet Navy. It was a significant job because of the close relationship between the US Navy and CIA on special collection programs. I was responsible for CIA officers cleared for some unique Navy-CIA collection activities and keeping senior CIA officials informed of new information about the Soviet Navy. This job was one of the best and I was thrown into the thick of things. The Soviet Navy was being expanded significantly, particularly the submarine force. The US Navy and CIA were aggressively pursuing collection programs aimed at following this strategic threat.

I enjoyed working with the Navy, particularly the submariners. They were always more open and welcoming than other the services. It helped that the new Deputy Director of CIA, Admiral Rufus Taylor, had been the Director of Naval Intelligence, which gave me great access to his former organization. He was a good leader and a real gentleman who took the time to give instructions, guidance, and criticism with a soft touch and real interest in his subordinates.

One of the first tasks he gave me was to prepare a paper on a new, radically different Soviet submarine. He wanted to show the report to Admiral Rickover who was scheduled to visit Admiral Taylor at the Agency. I was a bit out of my depth, but fortunately there were people inside the technical groups in CIA and the US Navy helping me put this together. Thankfully, it held up to the scrutiny of both admirals.

In 1968, a Soviet G-class submarine carrying nuclear missiles suffered a critical accident and sank while on patrol in the Pacific. The US Navy was able to pinpoint the exact location of the accident. I followed the Soviet efforts to locate the submarine. They apparently were never successful although both aircraft and surface ships searched the area. Knowing the location of the lost submarine allowed the CIA to begin a remarkable program to recover the submarine, possibly the most difficult technical effort supporting intelligence collection ever undertaken.

To avoid tipping off the Russians, the CIA worked with Howard Hughes under the guise that his company, Global Marine Development, was having the project constructed to extract manganese nodules from the ocean. Given Hughes's ability to attract attention, he informed the media of his plans and was so convincing that others considered taking on similar endeavors to obtain the elusive minerals. Thus, the USNS Hughes Glomar Explorer, renamed GSF Explorer, deep-sea platform was built undetected for Project Azorian, the effort to locate the Russian sub.

The Iran-Pakistan Adventure

In the fall of 1964, the Director of the CIA, in consultation with the President and the National Security Adviser, decided it was important to brief several foreign leaders on the Soviet strategic threat. The State Department was not enthused about the idea that the CIA would handle the briefings. At a session I attended at the State Department, the group made the decision not to send a briefer. John McCone came to the meeting late and indicated he had discussed the proposal with the president. The group changed its mind, and I was told to prepare the briefing and get visas for trips to Iran and Pakistan.

There were a number of more senior people who would have been fully capable of giving a briefing on Soviet military power. But Bruce Clarke and John Hicks tended to push junior analysts forward to test them and provide them with experience. I had been involved in a variety of activities involving Soviet strategic forces. I was an experienced briefer, knew the subject area, and was reasonably presentable. Bruce Clarke made the decision, with the approval of the Deputy Director of Intelligence, Ray Cline, and the DCI. My first trip abroad was going to be a doozy—briefing the Shah of Iran and the President of Pakistan.

Before I left, Bruce Clarke and the Director of Intelligence, Ray Cline, gave me some last-minute instructions that included clear guidance that I was not to let anyone other than the Shah and President of Pakistan sit in on the briefings. The last words from Bruce Clarke were, "Don't screw this up, Kerr."

A rather famous clandestine service officer—James Critchfield—who headed CIA operations in the Middle East and South Asia accompanied me. Our first stop was to brief the Shah of Iran in Tehran. Critchfield knew the Shah, and apparently needed no additional introduction. We walked up the steps of the palace and were met just inside the entry by the Shah. He was in civilian clothes—a suit and tie—and he was trim, handsome, polite, and welcoming. No one else was present, and we were escorted into a small sitting room. Jim Critchfield offered some comments about why the Director of CIA and President thought it necessary to provide this unique briefing on the Soviet strategic threat.

Before the briefing began, the Shah asked a servant to offer us something to drink. I was given a nearly full crystal glass of scotch without ice or water. I was not a regular drinker of hard liquor and took only a single, cautious sip. The briefing lasted about 40 minutes and included some questions from a clearly well-informed Shah. He was impressed by the photography showing details of the Soviet military forces.

The day after briefing the Shah, I flew to Karachi, Pakistan. The President of Pakistan was traveling, and I spent three days in Karachi waiting for the opportunity to brief him. Karachi was still crowded with refugees as a result of the war of independence. I had never seen anything like it, entire families living on the streets. I went out at night and wandered around, only to be told the next day that it was foolish to be outside after dark.

While in Karachi, I was invited to dinner with the CIA chief in Pakistan and was the honored guest at a first-class restaurant with a variety of senior Pakistani intelligence officers in attendance. Sitting at the table, I felt something crawling up my leg. I tried to ignore it, but when it reached my crotch, I could not stand it anymore. I jumped to my feet, unzipped by pants, reached inside and pulled out a huge cockroach. Throwing it on the floor, I stepped on it and sat down. Conversation at the table came to a halt and waiters and staff hurried over to calm the situation. As the most junior person in the room, I was thoroughly embarrassed and did not know whether to laugh or cry. So, I just picked up my fork and continued with lunch.

After a couple of days, President Ayub Khan decided that the briefing should be held in Rawalpindi. So off I went to the north of Pakistan. As it turned out, I had to wait another couple of days before giving the briefing. I was given a car and driver and decided to visit the ancient city of Taxila, which was captured by Alexander the Great during his romp through South Asia. Nothing remained of the city but ruins of some temples and the foundations of buildings. Along the road, a villager stopped me and asked if I wanted to buy a statue stored in a nearby hut. I took a look at an eight-foot Buddha carved in Greek style. It would not fit in my luggage. He offered to break off the head and sell it to me. I settled for an eight-inch statue of a frieze.

The next day I rode to the President's palace in Rawalpindi with the US Ambassador to Pakistan. President Ayub Khan was very distinguished-looking retired general who had assumed power in 1960. He had very little to say but seemed to listen carefully. Sitting next to the President was Ali Bhutto. I had been told that only the President was to be given the briefing, and I knew that Bhutto would be an unwelcome guest; he was pro-Russian and anti-US. I mentioned to the Ambassador that I had been instructed to give the briefing only to the President. He said he was not going to ask Bhutto to leave and told me to go ahead with the briefing. I did not think I was in a position to cancel the meeting, so I went ahead reluctantly.

The history of Pakistani leaders is bloody. Bhutto became President after Ayub Khan was ousted in a coup and hung by General Zia. I briefed—or more accurately, General Zia briefed me—on the Soviet threat in 1988. A bomb on his aircraft killed him and the US Ambassador shortly thereafter. In 1996, I briefed Ms. Bhutto not long before extremists killed her.

Work as an Analyst

I had some additional experiences working as a missile and naval analyst that expanded my horizon and offered valuable experience for the future. The CIA was a pioneer in space systems. It developed the first operational ability to take photographs from space and in the early 1960s operated a system that photographed huge areas of the Soviet Union and returned that film to earth. After the package of film was returned to earth, it went to the National Photographic Interpretation Center (NPIC), a part of the CIA. On a fairly regular basis, I was part of a small team of experts who went to the Center as the film was being exploited with the objective of quickly identifying key new information and providing an overall assessment of the mission. While I was the penman, real area experts provided the detailed analysis. The resulting assessment was sent to a few senior government officials.

It was a great opportunity to report on new military development in the USSR.

Another activity that became frequent, if irregular, was to accompany CIA directors to Congress for briefings describing the Soviet military threat. I helped draft the briefings, transport the equipment, run the presentation, and answer questions. Following one such briefing, Director McCone had a private one-on-one meeting with the Chairman of the Senate Armed Services, one of the most powerful people in Congress. I tried to excuse myself, but the Director insisted I attend. At that meeting the Director indicated that the Agency was about to begin a new program replacing the U-2 aircraft. He described the cost and capabilities of the plane. The senator indicated that he thought it was a great idea and approved the program. When asked if he should inform the minority leader of the committee, the senator said there was no need; he approved. A different time, a powerful senator.

Admiral "Red" Raborn became Director in 1965. He was not suited to head the Intelligence Community. Appointed by President Johnson, he had been the program manager for the Polaris Missile. He had a surprising lack of geographic knowledge for an admiral. I was one of his morning briefers, and he once asked if Libya was landlocked. The answer was "not totally."

I accompanied the admiral to several Congressional briefings. The first time he went to the Hill, he was concerned about the possibility of listening devices in the large chandeliers in the hearing room. Although reassured that the room had been swept by CIA technicians, the admiral climbed on a chair with a wooden pointer in his hand and poked at a very large chandelier until it was swinging rather wildly.

There was a crisis of sorts at another briefing. The previous day, there had been a report that the CIA was funding student groups in Europe. The briefing was before the Senate Foreign Relations Committee headed by Senator Fulbright. The Agency was clandestinely funding students in trying to persuade them not to support the local communists, and the senator who sponsored the Fulbright program was not happy although he almost certainly been briefed on the activity. During that briefing a number of CIA "experts" who the Admiral had brought along began private conversations with senators and staff and it was not long before the room was in anarchy. When we returned to CIA headquarters, Deputy Director Helms got everyone together and gave strict instructions about who should and should not go to these briefings and who should answer questions.

I was a morning briefer for DCI Raborn. He was particularly interested in the details about tactical information on the Vietnam conflict; the number of bombing sorties and damaged assessment, subjects the Agency was not particularly expert on. One evening, the Director of Intelligence, Ray Cline, called me to his office and gave me an envelope that he asked to be delivered to the DCI at the briefing the next morning. He also said that I should leave immediately after delivering the note. Cline had little regard for Admiral Raborn and was not bashful saying so, and I suspected this note was some sort of an ultimatum. I gave my briefing, handed over the envelope, and started to leave. The Director said, "Sit down." He then opened what turned out to be a resignation letter. The DCI had several comments about Ray Cline.

Richard Helms replaced Raborn in June of 1966. Over the next couple of years, I went to a number of congressional briefings with Helms. I remember one briefing rather well. As the junior person, I stayed behind during lunch break to provide security for the room and briefing materials. During the break, I went around the room and looked at the notes various senators had written on their yellow pads—questions and comments they intended to ask at the end of the Director's briefing. I copied down all this information and wrote out some comments for the Director to use, calling back to the CIA operations center for answers I did not have. When the briefing resumed, I gave Director Helm a list of questions and answers. We were well prepared for Q&A, even with some vu-graphs to support answers. Maybe too well prepared as some of the answers to questions were too deft and vu-graphs up a bit too soon after the question was asked. In hindsight what I did was probably unwise. Maintaining good relations with Congress and their confidence in the Agency was more important than being able to quickly answer some question of the moment, but I was young and thought tactically not strategically.

Sailing

A fringe benefit of my job was that I stumbled into the sport of sailing. After joining the Agency, I found out that a fairly senior officer regularly sailed in races on the Chesapeake Bay and was looking for deck hands. I volunteered and ended up on the crew for several races. He planned to take his boat to Woods Hole in New England for the summer and asked if I would help crew. It was a great experience. When we arrived at Woods Hole, I thought we were pulling up to a hotel only to be told it was the home of the boat owner's mother-in-law. I found out he came from a very wealthy family. He even rented a private plane to take us back to Virginia.

Not long after that adventure I helped a fellow in my office bring a Cuban fishing boat down the inland waterway from New Jersey to the Chesapeake Bay. Several years later, friends in Great Falls asked my wife and I to join then on a sailing trip in the islands. This and a subsequent trip were great experiences and led to the purchase of a 32-foot Pearson on which we sailed the bay for about ten years. My wife was very understanding for the first few years but eventually became bored with slowly going back and forth over the same body of water.

1968-1970
US President: Lyndon B. Johnson
CIA Director: Richard Helms

In 1968, I was asked to take the senior analyst position at the CIA unit in Honolulu that supported the Pacific Command. The current representative had irritated the command and the front office was looking for someone who had worked with the military. It did not take more than one evening to decide that two years in Hawaii would be a great experience. I realized that out of sight and out of mind for two years would not necessarily enhance my resume, but I thought Bruce Clarke would look out for me.

My boss in Honolulu was a very senior operations officer who had held several major jobs in Europe. He was a good officer to work with and had excellent relations with

Admiral John McCain, the feisty commander of Pacific forces. We wrote several speeches for Admiral McCain, including one delivered at a conference of all the military area commanders.

The job in Hawaii was fairly routine. We provided considerable support to the war in Vietnam and Laos. Most of the work involved supporting the J-2 (Intelligence). General George Keegan was the J-2 when I arrived. He had been Intelligence Chief of the numbered Air Force that conducted the strategic bombing in Vietnam, and that among other things led him to a deep dislike for the CIA. The Agency consistently reported that the bombing of the Ho Chi Minh trail was doing less damage to the North Vietnamese supply system than the Air Force claimed. At one point, the Agency wrote that if all the trucks the Air Force claimed credit for destroying along the trail were added up, the number would exceed the entire truck production of the USSR General Keegan did not find such analysis endearing.

While in Hawaii, I took the opportunity to visit a senior agency official coming from the Far East to meet General Keegan for the first time. After berating us for some time, the General proceeded to say that the CIA and the two of us were either fools or knaves. He strongly disagreed with the Agency's analysis of the Vietnam War. The Agency visitor and I took strong exception, and what ensued was a serious and heated argument. What a way to start a new job! But as I found out later, General Keegan liked to argue and bully people. You could survive only if you argued back.

That year, we received a message from Vientiane, Laos, asking for someone to serve as a temporary reports officer during the expected yearly push by the Vietnamese into the Plaine de Jars. I volunteered. Hawaii was too quiet, and I wanted to see what the war was like. It was a great experience. I met some interesting people and learned a bit about the work in the field. Long Tien was a particularly unusual place. This village was the headquarters of the CIA element that supported Vang Pao and the Meo tribesmen fighting to hold on to Laos. It was an armed camp and at times had the atmosphere of an armed fraternity. People worked incredibly long hours, and when they stopped working, they played hard. I was in the briefing room when the Air Force commander and deputy from Udorn were being briefed on the war in Laos. The General asked the CIA officer in charge what military experience he had. He answered, "I was a non-commissioned officer in the army." I don't think the General was impressed.

I had a number of interesting experiences in Laos. One of the first was how flimsy the cover story was for people in the country. I had brought my tennis racket with me and the first free day I went to join the local club. The manager asked where I worked and I said AID, which was my cover. He said, "Oh, you are one of the CIA people." Even the flight to Long Tien on a C-130 loaded with fuel bladders was an adventure. To land, the pilot came over a ridge and looked down at the field with a huge rock cliff at the end of the runway. He flew over and returned three times before he was successful.

It was in Laos that I decided the US could not win the war in Vietnam. A North Vietnamese major had been captured and was being debriefed in Savannakhet. I was involved in the reporting. His story about spending most of his adult life fighting the French and the US and his determination to continue convinced me that the US just did not have the staying power to defeat the Vietnamese.

I returned to CIA headquarters as the Chief of the China/Far East Military Branch. The branch chief job in the Directorate of Intelligence was (and is) the principal learning experience in any officer's career. You had to deal with people and their strengths and weaknesses in person, not through panels or boards. What you did had a direct impact on their future and career. But the performance of the branch also affected your future, as it should. If you could not be a good branch chief, there would be serious question about further advancement. The product was considered to be yours, and you took the credit and the criticism.

The China Branch was a strong group with several junior officers who had real analytic skills and a few older hands with skill and considerable experience in the area. It was a productive group. One of the great coups of the branch was its early analysis that China's defense minister, Lin Pao, had defected and subsequently crashed in Mongolia. There was strong resistance to this analysis from the political analysts that followed China in the Office of Current Intelligence, but the persistence of several strong analysts in the Branch paid off. Following Chinese military developments in the early 1970s was a bit like watching grass grow, but following the twists and turns of North Korea kept the group on its toes.

1972
US President: Richard M. Nixon
CIA Directors: Richard Helms / James Schlesinger

While the China Branch Chief, I got involved in the planning for a new real-time imagery system. After helping with the requirements process for the program for a year or so, I recommended to my boss, Bruce Clarke, that the Agency needed a full-time group working on this program to develop the techniques for collection and analysis. Mr. Clarke said, "If you are so smart, you head a group dedicated to this activity." I really did not want to be involved in such a group out of the line. But in 1972, I found myself heading the Special Studies Group with representatives from the Central Intelligence Agency, the Defense Intelligence Agency, the National Security Agency, and the National Photographic Interpretation Center. For the next two years, I was engrossed in technical collection systems and the exploitation of the information they collected. It was a good experience that gave me some appreciation for CIA's Directorate of Science and Technology, its program managers, and the complicated process of managing technically innovative and very expensive programs through the perils of competing interests and programs.

In 1974, I was asked to join the staff of the Committee on Imagery Requirements and Exploitation (COMIREX) as deputy to Roland Inlow. Roland was a long-time military analyst and had become a leader in the collection and exploitation of imagery. A brilliant man, Roland often knew too much and was unable to make relatively simple decisions. I was not so burdened. I began to make decisions for him and then reveal these actions at a convenient time. For example, we had a large requirements staff and needed a new chief of the unit. After Roland worried about the problem for a few weeks,

I selected the individual and put him to work. One day, I brought him in to meet Roland and introduced him as the new Element Chief. Roland was a bit irritated but also relieved. COMIREX involved extensive work with all elements of the Intelligence Community and the military services. It was good experience for the jobs that followed.

In 1976, George H. W. Bush had asked Admiral Daniel Murphy to head the Intelligence Community Staff. The staff's primary responsibility was to organize and support the activities of the DCI that extended beyond the Central Intelligence Agency. The staff was responsible for oversight of all aspects of national intelligence collection and analysis but had particular responsibility for the budget of organizations involved in national intelligence—CIA, NSA, DIA, the NRO, INR and parts of the FBI, Energy and Commerce.

John McMahon, a long-time CIA officer who had started his career as a courier, was the deputy to Admiral Dan Murphy. I was asked to be the executive officer of the Intelligence Community Staff. I had never worked in a staff position, but as with previous experiences, it added significantly to my understanding of the intelligence business. John McMahon was another of those officers whom I considered a great mentor. He was both substantively strong and very effective as a manager. John McMahon was a treasure to watch in full swing. Once, aggravated by some action or inaction on the part of the budget group of the staff, he called them all into his office (with me as a quiet observer) and proceeded to chew them out using the most colorful language. He got so into the assault that he took his shoe off and threw it against the wall, knocking down a picture. His secretary rushed into the room suspecting a fight had broken out. Despite the theatrics, John had the respect and affection of everyone who worked for him. He was Mr. Integrity. He literally knew the names of thousands of employees from the top to the bottom of the organization. I probably learned more from John than any of my bosses other than Bruce Clarke.

McMahon had a taste for malapropisms. I recorded many of these during staff meetings where they were met with nodding heads. Everyone knew what he wanted done despite the somewhat confusing language. "They are worried that we are going to climb in their knickers and tell them how to suck eggs." This referred to someone suspicious of the motives of the staff. "Unless we bite that can of worms, we will end up with a bunch of weenies in our lap." That meant he wanted a problem solved. "The leading edge of the camel's nose." He used the phrase to refer to the Defense Department's attempt to usurp some DCI authority. At least he kept even mundane meetings interesting.

The lesson of these years did not become clear to me for some time. I learned a great deal about technical collection, particularly imagery collection. I also observed the considerable power and vision that industry and the CIA program managers exercised in producing sophisticated technology that revolutionized intelligence. Carl Duckett, Les Dirks, and Rutledge "Hap" Hazzard are some of the true heroes of intelligence. They led the DDS&T and program offices of the 1960s and 1970s. But there were an equal number of creative people in the private sector who were fully committed to making technical collection what it is today. Profit was important but not nearly as important as keeping the US secure by collecting intelligence. Analysis was critical, but not very good without hard data.

I stayed on the IC staff for a year after the presidential election in 1976. Admiral Stansfield Turner became the DCI and had a somewhat troubled time as leader of the CIA.

1978
US President: Jimmy Carter
CIA Director: Stansfield Turner

I was asked to be the Deputy Director of the Office of Regional and Political Affairs (ORPA) in 1978. That office was responsible for political analysis worldwide. The Directorate of Intelligence was in disarray during this period. It had adopted a *laissez-faire* approach to personnel, with analysts writing their own fitness reports as well as writing reports on the performance of their supervisors. There was little discipline and a tendency to let all the flowers bloom when it came to intelligence production. As a result, the products were uneven and a bit sloppy. The office did not do well during the revolution in Iran, although the blame for not understanding how fragile the Shah's position was could be spread rather broadly. I am not sure what impact I had on this office, but I knew that changes were needed there and elsewhere. I began to believe that the DDI's analytic abilities had dulled.

The office, the DCI, and the administration faced a major problem during my short tenure there. In mid-1979, the Shah of Iran was forced to flee his country. He was sick with cancer, his supporters and the Iranian military collapsed without a struggle, and President Carter was not inclined to support a dictator against a popular uprising. The CIA was often criticized for not predicting the Shah's demise. Of course, even the Shah did not see the collapse of his regime until the very end. There were a large number of CIA, State, and military observers in Iran during the final years of the regime, but they apparently listened to the Shah's supporter and not the "street" and religious leaders. The CIA would hear more from radicals in Iran.

After just over a year, I was selected as the Director of the Office of Current Operations where I got a chance to see if I could improve the daily intelligence product. I believe my old mentor Bruce Clarke was behind the appointment. That office was responsible for the current intelligence publications: The President's Daily Brief and the National Intelligence Daily. It also managed the production of all intelligence reports, managed foreign liaison, and housed editors and geographers. It was an exciting office and ran a bit the way I expect a daily newspaper might operate. Each day, articles were submitted or ordered up for the overnight publications. My deputy in the office was Peter Dixon Davis, a longtime analyst and senior officer. Dixon had been a child movie and radio performer. He had been a regular on such shows as *Date with Judy* and was the smart teenager on *The Jack Benny Show*. Even more fascinating for me, the diminutive Dixon had been a stand-in for Shirley Temple. Dixon became a very close friend during the tumultuous period that followed.

The routine for publishing current intelligence was challenging. The day was spent reviewing articles and cajoling analysts to write pieces that the editorial staff,

Dixon and I thought were needed. At about 1800h, we began a review of the material on hand for the President's Daily Brief (PDB). We published the PDB and its companion, the Current Intelligence Bulletin, every day but Sunday. The review meetings lasted into the evening with some of the proposed articles dropping out in the process and some being completely rewritten. Fortunately, the editorial staff was an outstanding group of senior analysts who had covered many critical national security problems. Dixon was a most demanding editor, and he would spend considerable time arguing about the appropriateness of a particular word. After 2000h, this could be a bit tedious.

All of the Presidents since Lyndon Johnson have received a morning publication assessing new developments, commenting on ongoing issues, and providing basic biographic and scheduling data on foreign leaders. Few Presidents provided much feedback to those who prepared their daily fare, so it was a bit hit or miss. Of course, the staff at the White House was often only too willing to tell us how to prepare the products. Late in the Carter Administration, we received a copy of the President's Daily Brief with a note written by the President. It complained about the articles and the presentation. There was little to go on and some of us thought it was a bit like pronouncements of the Delphic Oracle. Nevertheless, he was our primary customer and we overhauled the publication. The format and content were changed, and we tried to follow what we believed to be the President's schedule and interests more closely. But Carter's message was a bit like the story told about Director of the FBI, J. Edgar Hoover, who wrote on a memo sent to him, "watch the borders." The system reportedly responded by increasing activity along the Canadian and Mexican borders. What Hoover really wanted was to be more careful with the borders of memorandum sent to him.

There was no absence of significant subjects to write about during the Carter Administration. The Iranian revolution, the hostages, a world oil crisis, the Soviet invasion of Afghanistan and Soviet activity scattered throughout the world all provided grist for our mill. Like newspaper editors, we were most excited by crises and instability.

I knew a bit about the experiences of Alexander the Great and the British in Afghanistan. But when the Russians sent military forces into the country in 1979, it focused the attention of intelligence on the country. The invasion caused President Carter to cancel US participation in the Moscow Olympic Games and initiate a CIA-led covert action program to assist Afghan tribes in driving the Russians out.

I traveled to Afghanistan with Directors Casey and Webster on two trips to Pakistan to meet with tribal groups known as the mujahideen. I also made a trip to Pakistan in 1990, the year after the Russians pulled out of Afghanistan.

The CIA provided weapons, training, and other support to the resistance. Of particular value were the Stinger anti-aircraft missiles which were effectively used by the Afghans to down Russian fighter aircraft and helicopters.

During one of my trips, I had dinner with the leaders of the Afghan resistance. One of the most radical leaders asked me what the US would do when the Soviets were driven out of his country. I said, "We should leave and let Afghans settle their own problems without US help. US involvement was unwise in a country that dislikes foreign interference and where tribal rivalries were so strong." The Russians withdrew from Afghanistan in 1989, but peace did not come to the country.

PART II

LOS ANGELES

A few days after Ronald Reagan won the 1980 presidential election, I was winging my way from Dulles International Airport to Los Angeles. I was to begin briefing the President-elect each morning. As director of the staff that published the President's Daily Brief, I was the logical person to take on this task.

5.

BRIEFING THE PRESIDENT

1981
US President: Ronald Reagan
CIA Director: William Casey

The election of a new President is always a major event for the CIA—new bosses, new problems, uncertainty, and confusion. There was considerable concern about the Reagan Administration because some of the people coming with the new President had been associated with the Nixon era, a tough period for the Agency. We were preparing for change and as the director of the office that produced the President's Daily Brief (PDB), I was particularly anxious.

President Carter had directed that the PDB be made available immediately to the President-elect and the Vice President-elect. The first contact with the new team was with Richard Allen who was to be Reagan's first national security adviser. The process began almost immediately with a series of briefings held in Allen's Washington business office, in cars, and at the Madison Hotel over breakfast. The briefings entered a new phase when the President-elect and the Vice President-elect made their first visit to Washington in mid-November.

Allen set up a couple of meetings with President-elect Reagan at his Blair House quarters. At the same time, we began daily briefings for Vice President-elect Bush, who was staying around the corner at the Jackson Place townhouse. As the President-elect and Vice President-elect prepared to return to Los Angles and Houston, retrospectively, things took an interesting turn. Bush felt that it was imperative that the newly elected President receive daily briefings based on the PDB, and—even more important—that a professional intelligence officer be present to answer any questions, provide background information, and to follow up on whatever intelligence needs Reagan might have.

I wrote the following article for the unclassified edition of the "Studies in Intelligence Winter" (along with Peter Dixon Davis) about briefing the President:

The presidential election of 1980 was over, and it was the morning after. In CIA's Office of Current Operations, we knew that a new boss and a new set of customers had us in their sights. Ronald Reagan would be in the White House by the end of January, and a new team of national security officials would be calling the shots. The CIA would have a new Director of Central Intelligence (DCI). He would bring in a new deputy. There probably would be other new faces at the top of CIA, and a new set of staff weenies would appear as well.

We knew that in the confusion of changing administrations and establishing daily intelligence support at top levels of a wary new leadership might just as likely be resisted as welcomed. At the same time, this new group valued intelligence; the question was whether they thought the CIA was up to the task. Our experience with a number of administrations was that they started with the expectation that intelligence could solve every problem, or that it could not do anything right, and then moved to the opposite view. Then they settled down and vacillated from one extreme to the other.

We found out early that Vice President-elect Bush was pushing for a regular morning briefing for the new President. We were getting prepared and Bruce Clarke decided that I should do the briefings. In a meeting with him early on in the process, I was standing in front of him discussing how we would go about this. He looked at me and said, "Kerr, one thing you need to do is get a black belt to replace the brown one you are wearing with your blue suit." I had never been very fashion conscious.

Shortly after Reagan's takeoff that afternoon, a message from the plane arrived at CIA Headquarters. Ed Meese asked that a CIA briefer be prepared to present the PDB to the President-elect at his home in Pacific Palisades the following morning. A few hours later, after hurriedly arranging for the daily transmission of the PDB to an Agency facility in Los Angeles, Peter Dixon and I were on a plane to the West Coast with no idea of what to expect at Reagan's house in Pacific Palisades. A cast of thousands, Secret Service a mile deep, and a palace of a residence? No, nothing of the kind.

The CIA security officer supporting us had located the house the previous day. Driving up the narrow road to the residence, the only sign of something unusual was that the driveway was closed off. A modest house, looking a bit rundown, was the first impression. A Secret Service agent approached, and I showed him a CIA identification card, saying I was there to brief the President-elect. No passes, no searches, no questions, and no horse-holders.

I went into the recreation room on the lower floor and told a young woman in the makeshift office space that I was there for the intelligence briefing. A minute later, the future President came out in his bathrobe. We went into the breakfast area, and he introduced Mrs. Reagan. A small brown dog sat next to the table. It was very casual and domestic. Reagan offered coffee, and we went into the den. He read the PDB carefully, asking occasional questions, and then read the other material. We talked about the briefing process and what type of material he would like to see. He agreed that unless there was some pressing engagement, an early morning briefing would work best. The pattern was set. Dixon and I spent ten days there rotating the briefings of Reagan before he was inaugurated.

I was always a bit nervous each time it was my turn, particularly right before the briefing. I would arrive at his house by myself. Other than a few staff members milling about, the place seemed largely deserted. I found Reagan to be very friendly. He had a good sense of humor and was not in any rush to get through the briefings, although he sometimes had a houseful of people prepared to see him soon after. He patiently read the items I suggested were important and asked solid questions. He definitely took the briefings seriously, but his ease and sense of humor helped me to relax as the briefer.

The other principals I briefed during the first year or so of the Reagan Administration were quite different. Vice-

President Bush was always pleasant and asked a lot of questions. He was seldom in a hurry and also had a good sense of humor. His background in intelligence and foreign policy meant he did not require the background on issues that others depended on.

NCA Adviser Richard Allen was usually impatient to get the briefing over. His primary interest was to get ready to brief President Reagan. I did not personally brief Secretary of State Schultz but did talk with him later in weekly luncheons. My experience briefing senior officials was that they usually were interested because they knew that the President received the same information and that kept them up to date with him. They also were aware that the CIA had some unique intelligence, considerable clout, and access to the VP.

I approached briefing people the same way I dealt with intelligence issues. I watched them when others were briefing and noted how they reacted—bored, impatient to move on, what subjects they were interested in, what kind of questions they asked. Know the person you are talking to as well as the topic you are briefing and pay attention to how they react.

Perhaps the most interesting aspects of the briefing process were the relationships that developed with those we were briefing. Often during presentations, or while we waited during telephone calls or other visitations, we overheard conversations between Reagan or Bush and potential cabinet members or advisers. We listened to discussions of their strengths and weaknesses, complaints, and personal exchanges that clearly were not meant for outsiders. We also watched the courting process and the beginnings of what would become the pecking order for those around the President. During this two-month period, we began briefing the Secretary of Defense-designate Caspar Weinberger and Secretary of State-designate Alexander Haig.

By Inauguration Day, the daily briefing system was so well established that it seemed natural to all involved that it would simply continue. As career current intelligence practitioners, we were in the right place at the right time. And we had the best professional products in the business. If we deserve any plaudits for playing our roles well, we were quick to bow to an able supporting cast and to our indulgent customers.

The briefing process settled into a routine over the next year. Dixon and I rotated briefing the Secretary of State, the National Security Adviser and the Vice President. We would arrive at CIA Headquarters at about 0500, read the overnight take, review the PDB and add any new material that seemed appropriate. We went to the home of Secretary Haig and then rode to the State Department in the Secretary's limo. We had about 30 minutes for his briefing. Secretary Haig always had comments on the PDB, often critical or at least disagreeing with some of the analyses, particularly items concerning terrorism. There were often spirited discussions and disputes but usually predictable and in good spirit. Leaving the State Department, we then usually went to the Vice President's residence at the Naval Observatory on Mass Avenue. That briefing also lasted about 30 minutes unless the VP had a number of questions, and then we were off to the White House to brief the National Security Advisor (who would then brief the President). Other members of the PDB staff briefed the Secretary of Defense.

The briefing process took a good deal of time and effort but was worth it in many ways. We got immediate feedback on our product and clear guidance on what our customers wanted and needed. I believe most of them grew more confident in the quality and responsiveness of the Agency and its product. We could not ask for more than that: a critical and involved customer. One aside: briefers of senior government officials tended to be treated differently than normal people. Conversations not meant to be overheard by others were commonly held in their presence, and they were expected to keep those confidences. Dixon Davis and I agreed early on that the only thing we would report on was substantive questions or comments, not gossip or information irrelevant to our mission.

Reorganizing the Directorate of Intelligence

In 1982, John McMahon became the Deputy Director for Intelligence, the analytic arm of CIA. It was not long before McMahon became frustrated with the directorate. Every time he wanted information on a particular country, or subject half a dozen people would show up. It was not easy to get a single view from a political analyst, a military analyst, and an economic analyst. He decided to reorganize the directorate along geographic rather than functional lines. This made a lot of sense because most of the CIA's customers—the State Department, the unified and specified commands and even the National Security Council—were organized in that manner.

While McMahon solved one problem—getting all the analysts working on a particular country together in one office. But he created a new problem. Focusing on countries or regions meant that offices that followed economic, military or scientific issues crossing country lines were abolished, or at least their analysts were spread out across the directorate with small staffs left to following these functional areas. The result was that the Agency's expertise in these areas diminished rapidly.

One of CIA's real strengths was its depth of knowledge and expertise on foreign military. Not just numbers of tanks and missiles but how those weapons would be used in actual combat. Detailed economic analysis on foreign economies and technical data on missiles, and radar was slowly lost only to be replaced by general and sometimes fluffy analysis on politics.

At one point in the planning for the new organizational structure, McMahon showed me a list of proposed officer directors and asked my opinion. I was not enthused about the nominee for Director of the Office of East Asia Analysis and told him so. A few days later he came back to me and said, "You did not like the nominee for this office, so I have decided to make you the director." I should have remembered my army lesson to keep my mouth shut.

I had no expectations of moving to another job, and I was a bit disappointed to no longer be rubbing shoulders with the leaders of the government. However, I enjoyed running a large office working on important countries. For one thing, it meant organizing a new office from pieces of several other groups who worked the Far East but had been organized along functional lines—economic, political, military, and scientific.

A good deal of my time in the East Asian Office was spent trying to merge the three functional offices. We had too many economists and military analysts working marginal issues in China. My deputy in the office was Jim McCullough. He was an old friend who had been involved in the briefings for President Reagan and the cabinet and was an experienced hand at following the Far East.

The East Asian Office was a busy place with responsibility for the Far East and Southeast Asia. China, Japan, South and North Korea were the focal points but during my tenure, the Philippines was a key area of concern.

One time, Jim McCullough and I were hosting the head of the South Korean Intelligence service and his staff at the Four Seasons Hotel in Georgetown. During the dinner, we found out that the Vice President was hosting a dinner in the adjacent dining room. I barged into his dinner and asked him if he would say a few words to my Korean guests. Without any hesitation, he spent several minutes talking to them. The delegation was overwhelmed that the Vice President of the United States would leave his guests to talk with them. That visit guaranteed the cooperation of the Korean service for years.

Outside of work, I found that Great Falls, Virginia, was a great place to raise children and make friends. Because I was a bit older than some of my fellow analysts at CIA and had a large family, I did not get heavily involved in their social activities. Consequently, most of Jan's and my friends were locals from Great Falls—neighbors, people with children the age of ours and, as it turned out, tennis players.

Great Falls was an interesting mix of people. Some had moved into the area to get out of the city, some lived there because they could not afford to live closer to town, and many wanted the privacy of larger acreage. Some had families that had lived in the area for generations. It was a good combination of the wealthy and middle-class. It was the sort of close community where if a friend saw your children doing something stupid, they would say something to them, and the children would pay attention. It was a tight area and events ranged from Boy Scouts and regular square dancing to little league baseball and local parties.

I found the people in Great Falls fun to be around, and that led to many interesting experiences. One event was particularly amusing and showed just how willing our friends were to engage in a bit of silliness.

Several neighbors were sitting on a grassy knoll along a historic road in Great Falls, Virginia. In fact, five of us were drinking wine and having a wonderful Sunday afternoon. Our conversation turned to the brochure we had all received the previous day giving notice that the Catholic Church was sponsoring a fine-home tour for charity. The tour was going to several high-class houses in the area. Cocktails and appetizers would be served at one house, and the host would give guests a tour of the 14,000-square-foot residence that included an indoor pool and greenhouse. At the second house, a nice gourmet dinner would be served, and guests given a music presentation by a well-known pianist. The third house would feature an assortment of desserts prepared by a local chef and there would be a showing of paintings and sculptures that had been collected from around the world. Door prizes would include a dinner prepared for four, tickets to the Kennedy Center and one surprise gift.

Vintage wine was to be served at all the houses. The cost of the Greater Great Falls House Tour was $100.

The *hoi polloi* seated on the grassy knoll decided immediately that this house tour sounded a bit too pretentious and a bit over the top. We needed some response to puncture the balloon. The idea of a "Great Falls Lesser Home Tour" was hatched and preparations began.

The group decided to open their houses for the tour and invite all of their "low class" friends. The format followed that of the Catholic-organized home tour and we also developed a brochure. At the first house on our tour, we served saltine crackers with Cheez Whiz and Vienna sausages. That home featured a display of garden tools, many of them broken and rusted. The second house served navy beans and corn bread, and the attraction was a collection of dust bunnies and a large basket of single socks. At the third and final house, the dessert was Moon Pies and Jell-O with marshmallows and a display of half-finished, hastily assembled crafts. Ripple wine was served at all the houses. The cost listed in the tour brochure was $1.24.

To add a little mystery to the event, people were told to assemble in a local church parking lot where they would be picked up and transported to unidentified houses. We also indicated that there was a "mystery" house included on the tour. There would be door prizes—a check of tires and free air from a local gas station, two gallons of gas from Buck's Country Store, and a single plant from a local nursery.

An interesting aspect of the tour was how many people came not knowing what this was all about or where they were going. At one point late in the evening, one guest asked if the "mystery" house was her house and after being reassured that there was no "mystery" house, she called her mother and said she could go to bed because no one would be coming for a visit.

Jan and I also returned West every other year to visit family and renew our populist ties. We often attended Roseburg High School reunions. At one of them, a group got together and decided it would be fun to regularly meet at various places around the country. Our first trip was to Nevada to visit a couple who lived in the desert. Most arrived in campers or RVs and parked in a circle around the small house. Late in the evening, after a night of revelry, our group tried to fold some chairs and put them back in an RV. We could not figure out how to make them fit and it became comedic. The group took the name "chairs" from that incident and in subsequent years we met in Bend, Oregon; Reno, Nevada; Honolulu, Hawaii; Branson, Missouri; the Outer Banks, North Carolina; Roseburg, Oregon; Las Vegas, Nevada; and Eugene, Oregon. Well-traveled, indeed.

Managing the Directorate of Intelligence

In 1986, Robert M. Gates replaced John McMahon as the Director of Intelligence. He revolutionized the directorate by insisting on a tightly reviewed product using a very interventionist approach to manage the production of intelligence. It was a bit of a shock to the analysts and managers alike. Some argued that he politicized intelligence by introducing his views into key products. Others were excited about his hands-on approach. When the position of Associate Deputy Director for Intelligence opened up in July 1982, Gates asked me to take the job.

I served as the Associate Deputy Director for Intelligence until December 1985, and after a four-month tour as the Deputy Director for Administration, returned as Deputy Director for Intelligence, staying in that job until March of 1989. These jobs were the ultimate positions for analysts. Organizing the research program for the production of finished intelligence and monitoring current intelligence products, responding to questions from policymakers, briefing the congressional oversight committees, and supervising the most extensive and impressive groups of analysts in the US government was a daunting task. What was not to like about that? Gates also gave me the tasks of working with the other intelligence agencies and collection committees and staying in touch with the DCI advisory committees. The only thing better than being the Associate Deputy Director of Intelligence was being the Deputy Director. I got to do both.

The nearly four years as Gates' deputy were interesting, educational, and busy. He was a demanding leader of the directorate. The two of us reviewed every paper produced in the directorate as well as the President's Daily Brief. Gates was relentless in trying to improve the responsiveness of intelligence to the policymaker. He intimidated some managers and analysts and expected them to defend their analysis. Some found the pressure a bit too much and others thought he was trying to shape the product to his own liking.

I often found myself in the position of trying to moderate his impatience and protect those I thought were innocent but unwise. I spent a lot of time trying to convince analysts and managers to pay attention to what he was trying to do and not to do something really stupid. There was a lot of tension between Gates and the directorate, and I believe that one of my real accomplishments was as the middleman in the process. I became very fond of Gates. He had a great sense of humor and a keen mind. He was ambitious and impatient, but the product that came out of the directorate during this period was relevant, concise, and defensible.

During that time, I hired a secretary named Susan Shiff to work in the front office of the Directorate of Intelligence. Initially, the position seemed to be a challenge for her, but I was used to hiring based on my instincts and felt she would grow into the position and make it her own, which is exactly what happened. After all, I was in the same situation. My position was a bit of a challenge, but I would grow into it. Over time, we not only became great working partners but wonderful friends as well. As the years went on, my wife Jan used to joke with her about being my "day wife" since we often spent 12-hour days together, week after week, managing one event after another.

Susan was in the Directorate of Intelligence office for four years before she became my Special Assistant when I became the Deputy Director of Central Intelligence (DDCI) and Acting Director of Central Intelligence.

Becoming Deputy Director of Administration

In January 1986, DCI Casey decided he wanted someone with analytic experience to run the Directorate of Administration when the current director, Harry Fitzwater, retired. I was his choice. I remember asking him at the time about the wisdom of the appointment given my lack of experience in any of the directorate's areas of responsibility. He said, in no uncertain terms, that was what he wanted to do.

As Director of Administration, my job was to run the full range of support activities for the Agency—security, personnel, communications, training, and data processing among others. It was a complicated and difficult set of tasks made even more difficult because what it did overseas had to protect officers serving under cover and conducting activities that needed to remain in secrecy.

Imagine trying to support officers who were not connected to an official US organization in a foreign country, particularly a hostile country. To place an officer in such a position requires secrecy in recruitment, training, and location. Everything associated with that individual needs to be protected: pay, retirement, health insurance programs, and communications. Things we take for granted cannot escape detection even from a modestly competent hostile intelligence organization. That is the challenge of CIA administrative directorate in its support of operations.

Just after my promotion, Bill Casey had a retirement party for Harry Fitzwater. Harry was very proud that he had been instrumental in getting approval for a new building that was to be built next to the original headquarters building. A large bronze plaque temporarily placed in the hall of the old building listed his name as one of the key people involved in getting the funds and approval for the new building. I decided to play a joke on Harry and had our photographer take a picture of the plaque with me standing next to it. A graphics expert then replaced Harry's name with mine. Bill Casey presented the altered picture to Harry during his party with a comment something to the effect of, "Now that Dick was taking the job, it seemed only fair that he should have his name on the plaque." Harry was not amused until he recognized that this was all a joke at his expense.

To say I was overwhelmed by the new job is an understatement. Fortunately, I had a wonderful deputy who would have been a better choice to head the directorate. He was very generous in helping me learn the ropes and trying to master the complexity of the job. I also credit the heads of the various offices in the Directorate for being very patient and trying to help a real novice, not take advantage of my inexperience.

When Robert Gates was selected as Deputy Director of the Agency, I was moved back to take his job. I felt much more comfortable as the Director of Intelligence. My positions as Associate and then Deputy for Intelligence during the period of 1982 to 1989 were satisfying and remarkably diverse. As ADDI and DDI, I represented the Intelligence Community on the NSC planning group that developed and recommended policy to the NSC. During this period, we also started a weekly briefing for one of our oversight committees—The House Permanent Select Committee for Intelligence. A very successful venture, it helped keep the Congress from being surprised by activities or analysis.

There is nothing the oversight committees disliked more than surprises that raised questions about the quality of their oversight. The major problem was that it required discipline on the part of members to listen to someone else for one hour. It also required that the CIA briefing be both interesting and useful. Not surprising, the House briefings only lasted for a couple of years before being stopped by a new chairman. The Senate Select Committee for Intelligence expressed interest in having a similar weekly briefing but could not find enough time to organize even one. I found that I liked testifying before the oversight committees, as strange as that sounds. My relations with committee members was mostly very good, and I believed the oversight process offered valuable protection to the Agency which did not have a strong constituency like the military services or the FBI. Several of the staff directors of the committees remain good friends.

In 1988, my trip to Asia were filled with new adventures. After a stop in Guam, our group went on to Japan, but China, the next stop, was the most interesting. We landed at Beijing airport in a huge US Air Force plane painted khaki and emblazoned with a large American flag on the tail. Hardly a secret appearance. We were put up in a large guest house and taken to various historical sites—the Great Wall, the Forbidden City where someone rushed up and loudly shouted out, "Hey, Bill!" It was apparently a friend from St. Louis who was quickly surrounded by our security people and rushed away.

It was an interesting meeting with Chinese intelligence. We were taken to Xi'an to see the soldiers in the covered tomb. On the trip north, an old man on a bicycle was beaten on the shoulders because he did not get out of the road quickly enough. In Xi'an we ate lunch with the Regional Military Commander. I was given camel tendon soup which was like eating a rubber band. I always wondered if the Chinese were testing Westerners to see just what outrageous things they would eat. Just as we were leaving for home, the Chinese insisted on coming aboard our aircraft to make sure we were not smuggling a Chinese dissident who had been hiding in the US Embassy for months. We had some large cases aboard that the police insisted we open.

I was inclined to wait the Chinese out and not let them inspect our airplane, but wiser heads prevailed. From China, we went to Pakistan. It was my third visit to that country and two more would follow. We had a very interesting discussion with President Zia. He spent time in Jordan during Black September when the Palestinians were trying to overthrow the King of Jordan and became a close friend of Hussein. President Zia gave us a long, rather eccentric talk about the Soviet threat complete with maps.

Obviously, we spent time talking about support to the tribes in Afghanistan fighting the Soviets. Zia, the longest serving President of Pakistan, was impressive. It was disturbing to learn that he was killed not long after our visit when his airplane crashed, likely caused by a bomb aboard.

Our party spent a fair amount of time at training camps along the Afghan border. At one dinner, I sat next to Gulbadin Hekmatar, the leader of a faction that was anti-West and anti-Soviet. During the dinner he asked me what the US would do after the Soviets were forced out of Afghanistan. Very undiplomatically, I said the US would have little or no interest in Afghanistan after the Soviet left.

We went to the Khyber Pass and had dinner with the Khyber Rifles at their fort. It was an interesting dinner with a large barbecued fat-tailed sheep placed in the center of the table. You simply sliced off your portion. Bill was given the tail, the choicest piece. We went on to India. This was a period during which there was some serious tension along the Pakistan-India border and in Kashmir. Some thought it could lead to war and even the use of nuclear weapons. India was amazing, with cows wandering in the street, snake performers on every corner, and bright colors everywhere. We went to the Pink Fort and rode elephants up the road. Looking down, I saw an interesting sight, an elephant was standing with its feet in the dirt and covered by a large tent. I was told that the animal had broken its foot and to immobilize it, they had it stand in holes with the broken foot covered in concrete.

One time, a national security meeting had been scheduled in the Situation Room. Both Bill Casey and Bob Gates were unavailable, so I filled in. It was an interesting experience with Vice President Bush, Secretary of Defense Cheney, National Security Adviser Scowcroft, Director of the FBI, and a couple of other cabinet members sitting around the small table. And then there was me. Secretary Weinburger arrived late and someone—I believe it was the VP—had lowered Caspar's chair as close to the floor as possible. The President and the Defense Secretary arrived at about the same time, and when Weinburger sat down, his head barely came to the level of the table. There was some laughter from other cabinet members, and the President made an amusing comment. I sat quietly wondering how in the world I ended up there.

Other momentous and varied events over those seven years included Nicaragua, Afghanistan, the US hostages in Lebanon, the Iraq-Iran War, Iran-Contra, escorting of tankers in the Persian Gulf, terrorism, the beginning of the Panama Crisis, South Africa, China, Grenada, arms control, and most important, the beginning of the end of the Soviet Union. It was a heady time when intelligence played a key international role. Most of these crises—Grenada and Libya were exceptions—did not involve the direct use of US military forces. Intelligence was a critical player in these years. It was often a more integral component than the US military. In fact, it often was more "operational"—in Afghanistan and Nicaragua for example—than the US military. However, things were going to change, and it was not too many years before it seemed like the only solution to any national security problem was to deploy operational forces.

Although the CIA and the other elements of the Intelligence Community played a significant part in US policy during the 1980s, it was by no means a neat and simple process. Sometimes the CIA got itself in the position of torpedoing policy because of its analysis and reporting, and particularly its briefings to Congress.

An excellent example of this problem involved the US decision to flag and escort tankers in the Persian Gulf. The Intelligence Community judged that this action would draw fire from the Iranians including terrorism, direct attacks on the tankers and escorts, and perhaps even mining. Frank Carlucci, the National Security Adviser, and General Colin Powell, the Deputy National Security Adviser, were unhappy with our analysis and particularly with our briefings to the Hill. They believed—and were of course right—that we were giving ammunition to those who opposed the policy. At one meeting I attended with Tom Wolfe, a senior Middle East Analyst, Carlucci commented, "You are not being particularly helpful." My response was that good intelligence was not always helpful.

Powell seldom neglected to mention his irritation at the role of intelligence in this event. My reaction, now and then, was that both policy and intelligence had done exactly what they should have done. Intelligence laid out its concerns about the implications of a policy, and policymakers took whatever steps they could to prepare for various contingencies. As it turned out, most of the concerns of intelligence actually came true. Because of its warnings, the US was in a position to counter them.

Other conflicts between intelligence and policymakers were not uncommon. The White House and William Casey were adamant about driving the Sandinistas from power in Nicaragua. CIA created the Contra military force to achieve that policy objective. Many in Congress strongly opposed this policy.

There is no doubt that the Contras put pressure on the government that ultimately led to an election and the Sandinista defeat at the polls. However, there was a major disagreement between the DDI and those running the program about how successful the Contras were in prosecuting the war. The Nicaraguan analysts in the DDI were convinced that the operators were putting too glossy a finish on their reporting, and they were equally certain that the Contras could not win a war with the Sandinistas.

This particular issue highlighted the problem of conducting a covert operation and providing the report card on the effectiveness of that operation. In this case, neither the White House nor the DCI wanted to hear negative views about the progress of the war. The analysts in the DI stuck to their guns and presented them anyway, which resulted in a constant flow of "objective" reporting that tried to place the Contra activity in context. Bill Casey was not happy with this reporting but did not try to stop it. He did express his disagreement and often sent his own communications to the White House to counter analysis produced in his own current intelligence publications.

One of the most dramatic events during this period was what came to be called the Iran-Contra Scandal. Too much has already been written on this subject, and I will relate only my personal involvement. The CIA had a strong analytic group following both Iran and Iraq. There was general agreement among the analysts that there was not a "moderate" group inside Iran that might be open to negotiations about the hostages being held in Lebanon. Oliver North's initiative to open discussions with the Iranians, provide them some intelligence on Iraq, and sell some weapons was initiated without any input from the DI analysts. Just before Oliver North's flight to Teheran, I was asked to provide some information on Iraqi military deployments that could be passed to the Iranians. After checking with the DCI and being reassured that this was an approved US policy effort, a package was developed that provided some general intelligence but contained few specifics that would be militarily significant.

Shortly thereafter, I went to see Bill Casey and expressed my concern that we were embarked on a very dangerous course in supporting both Iran and Iraq. Casey listened and asked me to prepare him a short memorandum on the subject, but my concerns obviously came to nothing.

Shortly after this incident, an officer who had access

to some very sensitive reporting told me that there was some reason to believe that money obtained from Iranian arms sale purchases was being used to fund the Contras in Nicaragua. Few details were available, but I decided that I would at least pass on the information to Bob Gates, who was the Deputy Director at that time.

I went to his office and in a casual conversation mentioned what I had been told. After the Iran-Contra affair became public knowledge, I gave a written statement about this event after being questioned about any involvement I had with this issue by a lawyer investigating the affair. When Bob Gates was going through his first confirmation hearing, he said he did not recall the conversation. I was asked to testify during the hearing and repeated my experience but added that I regularly popped into his office and talked with Bob about all sorts of issues.

Obviously, working for Bill Casey was an interesting experience. I was never a close confidant, but clearly, he had enough trust in me to make me the director of two of the four directorates in the CIA. My first contacts with Mr. Casey came during the transition between the Carter and Reagan Administrations, but these were infrequent and not substantive. After he was sworn in as DCI, he made few personnel changes, but he did get rid of the transition team that had proposed some radical changes to the Agency. He knew what he wanted to do with the CIA, make it an aggressive and effective instrument of policy.

The first several months of the Casey period were a bit chaotic. Few of us understood his priorities. He was action oriented and wanted to attack the Soviet Union on every issue and every battlefield. The CIA and particularly the Directorate of Intelligence did some great analysis on military, political, and economic developments. It was far less comfortable offering opinions about how to change the situation. It was not an action organization. Conversations with Casey were difficult, partly because he mumbled. It was not unusual to ask him to repeat himself several times. At about the third request, he could become really cranky. Even when clearly understood, his activism was foreign to CIA, particularly the DDI.

Casey's dislike of congressional oversight of intelligence was apparent to all, including the Congress. The on-and-off financial support approved by the Congress for Nicaragua and inclination to distrust Casey and therefore the Agency led to a level of oversight that was intrusive and maddening to the DCI.

Casey brought a vigor and excitement to the CIA that had been missing. He had access to all the key players in government and some of his influence perked down to those who worked for him. He also made some important enemies. As the DDI, I regularly attended a lunch with Secretary Shultz, Under Secretary Bob Kimmitt, and Casey. Those lunches sometimes began with Casey asking Shultz why he did not fire the State Department officer responsible for Africa who was actively pursuing a settlement in Angola that Casey disagreed with. Bob Kimmitt and I usually sat quietly, speaking only when asked a question. We were not about to get between these two growling bears. These lunches were not relaxing, pleasant affairs that involved polite chitchat. They were contentious and prickly but never boring.

Casey's clout as Director of CIA passed down to people

in the organization. For example, as the Associate Deputy, I had no difficulty getting collection organizations to respond to tasking or a request for information or assistance. The Intelligence Community knew that I spoke for William Casey, and no one questioned his authority.

When Casey died in 1987, Gates was nominated as the Director of Central Intelligence. But after a long and tortuous confirmation hearing, the shades of Iran-Contra and testimony from several critics in CIA, his name was withdrawn, and he stayed in the position of Deputy Director.

In 1987, Judge William Webster was nominated as the DCI. Webster was the Director of the FBI and came to the job with a reputation for integrity and competence. When I heard that he had been nominated as the DCI, I called a contact in the Bureau. He said in no uncertain terms that CIA was in for some rocky times. He described Webster as a tough taskmaster who was very difficult to work for.

I was directly involved with Judge Webster from the moment he became DCI. The problems of intelligence did not start or end with a new director. Shortly after his confirmation, I needed to prepare him for a very contentious NSC meeting addressing the US decision to escort foreign tankers in the Gulf. I traveled with him on two foreign trips, including one to Pakistan that focused on the Afghan War. We developed a close and easy relationship. I was never excluded from any meeting and felt comfortable opening the door between our offices and talking to him at any time. He gave me a great deal of independence, and we became more than just boss and deputy.

Once I went into his office only to be introduced to

the Judds, the mother and daughter country singing duo. The Director and I were scheduled to go to an awards ceremony, and we asked the two singers to join us. It was an unusual presentation that would have been more interesting if there had been music.

I was never sure what to call Judge William Webster. "Judge" seemed a bit awkward, particularly in the CIA which broke the law in foreign countries. "Bill" was just too casual and informal. For a while I just referred to him as "boss," but that seemed a bit silly. In the end, the appellation just varied with the setting. In formal meetings, it was "Director." Inside the CIA, it was "DCI."

Director Webster was not a foreign policy expert or junkie. When faced with a major issue or crisis, he developed a good command of the substance and never shrank from hard decisions or holding a contrary view. He had particularly good judgment when matching people to jobs inside the Agency. He was very sensitive about any personal attacks in the press and would not rest until he had corrected the record. I learned from him that it was important to let no accusation go unanswered. It was important to have your version of the issue on the record.

Bill Webster saved the CIA a good deal of pain when he became DCI. Casey had made a lot of enemies and some of that antagonism was almost certainly going to be directed toward the Agency when he was no longer present to defend it. Webster's presence provided a good shield. He was above reproach and made a difficult target.

Bob Gates had to wait for the election of George Bush before being appointed Director of Central Intelligence. And I had to wait until that event before moving to the position of Deputy Director of CIA.

The Deputy Director of CIA

On the morning of December 28, 1989, my assistant, Sue, buzzed and said that I had a call from Air Force One. I picked up the phone and someone said, "Hold for the President-elect." Bush came on and said he would like me to accept the position as the Deputy Director of Central Intelligence. A bit flustered and surprised, I said I would be honored and was excited to work for him. He said he was glad I was there to take the job and looked forward to working with me. What a way to start the day!

As soon as I could catch my breath, I went down the hall to talk with Judge Webster. Obviously, it had been his recommendation that led to my nomination. I assumed that Gates, who already had been selected by Bush to be the Deputy National Security Adviser, weighed in as well.

I continued to serve as the deputy for intelligence over the next two months and began filling out the forms and various things expected of a presidential nominee. That included courtesy calls on members of the two Congressional oversight committees. One thing struck me about this process. No one asked me what party I belonged to or any of the other litmus questions that now seem an accepted part of the process. I filled out the forms declaring income and investments. As McMahon said about this process when he was nominated, "It was embarrassing to have accumulated so little in an entire career."

The confirmation process was a bit tedious. Nevertheless, it was not the destructive proceeding that seems to be the norm today. I was given a set of questions from the Senate Select Committee that was responsible for conducting the confirmation hearing and making a recommendation to the full Senate.

In February 1989, I went to the large hearing room in the Senate office building accompanied by my wife and daughter and a group of CIA lawyers. The hearing took most of the morning and was heavily slanted toward how I saw my responsibilities with regard to oversight by the Congress.

It was not all sunshine and roses. Senator Metzenbaum, who was not a friend of the CIA, had sent me a large number of questions. Many were in the category of, "When did you stop beating your mother?" When I got the long list of questions from the Senator, I was a bit irritated. I knew his staff had just pulled out the routine concerns and accusations. Consequently, I answered most of them with a terse "yes" or "no." Senator Metzenbaum voted against my nomination in the full Senate vote and indicated in the record that I had not been fully responsive to his questions. It is probably a bit childish, but I was pleased that he did not vote for me.

My wife and daughter were outraged by the conduct of the senators during the hearing. The senators asked questions and then got up and left the room before hearing the answers. They talked to staff and each other during questioning even if they had asked the question. They seemed to wander in and out of the hearing room. I did not see anything unusual about their conduct, but I had been in hearings before.

All in all, the hearing went rather well. Within a few days, there was a full affirmative vote in the full Senate. I heard that the Senate had actually confirmed me in March. I wanted to be sworn in immediately, because there was a lot of work to be done. Sue found a notary in the Agency credit union. Marion Rygiel did the honors. I was sworn in.

A formal swearing in was held in the Indian Treaty Room of the Old Executive Office Building next to the White House. Judge Webster asked Justice Warren Burger to officiate. General Scowcroft and Bob Gates arranged for the President to attend the ceremony. A variety of guests—my family, personal friends, colleagues, and members of the Intelligence Community—attended. It was unusual to have such pomp and ceremony for the deputy of an agency, but it was a great honor.

I came to the job with many of the same feelings of apprehension and excitement that I experienced when taking on previous assignments. No one can fully understand the responsibilities or pressures of a particular job until they are there. I was confident in myself and in the organization. I knew there were smart people around me, and they would keep me on track. I knew that I could learn even if I did not know it all at the time. Fortunately, Sue Shiff was there to keep me on the straight and narrow.

The next three years were a sweep through some of the momentous changes in the 20th century. My first priority was to provide the best possible intelligence to the CIA's customers. This meant trying to understand the issues and how intelligence could be both objective and helpful. Second, I was very concerned that the CIA was being placed in the position of just one of several intelligence organizations, not the "Central" organization that in my view it should be. Third, I took seriously the responsibilities for the budget and programs of the other intelligence agencies and organizations.

I knew all of the senior people in the CIA and most of

those in other agencies and departments. I had worked for several years with the Director of Operations, Dick Stolz and John Helgerson, who took my place as the Director of Intelligence. The Director of Administration was an old friend and colleague, Rae Huffstutler. Helaine Boater was the Comptroller, and I had been her deputy in the office responsible for political and regional analysis. I had worked for, and with, the Deputy Director for Science and Technology, Evan Hineman. In addition, having worked in several different offices and staffs, I had worked directly with many officers throughout the CIA. My stay on the Intelligence Community Staff and work on technical collection gave me another set of contacts outside the CIA building. I knew the Director of the National Security Agency and the head of DIA, as well as the Director of the NRO. All in all, it was a comfortable fit even if the tasks ahead were going to be challenging.

Before being nominated as Deputy Director of CIA, I had made a commitment to my wife that I could not back out of. Jan's parents had invited us to go to the Oberammergau Passion Play with a group of Catholics from Oregon. I had agreed, but that was before becoming DDCI. Bill Webster had no problem with my trip, although it came at a difficult time.

The Agency decided that I could go, but only if accompanied by some security officers. Dan and Jack drew the short straws and accompanied a bus load of Oregonians for more than a week under the cover that they were nephews of my in-laws.

The whole affair turned out to be a great adventure. Starting in Paris, we traveled to Switzerland and Germany and the play. I was skeptical about seeing the Passion Play, but it was spectacular, ending with the crucifixion and resurrection of Christ taking place during an impressive real-life storm with dramatic lightning. The group went on into East Germany where the gates were open without guards. On to Leipzig and then Rostock and escaping from East Germany to Denmark and home.

Our trip came at a time when the Soviet empire was crumbling. There was considerable confusion in Germany in 1989 as borders were opened. When our bus got to the East German border, the gates were wide open and no guards present. Our guide was as baffled as we were. We met some confused guards when we were leaving East Germany in Rostock. They expected to see passports that had authorization for entry into the East. It took a couple of bottles of wine and some cheese to convince them to let us board the ship for our next destination—Copenhagen.

In Paris and East Germany, we knew that someone was following us. Jan had worked for CIA training officers to pick up on surveillance. She and the two security officers kept careful track of our "watchers." At one point in Leipzig, it was clear that an individual taking photographs was spending far too much time taking pictures of us. We never knew whether it was a "friendly" service making sure nothing happened to us, or someone "less friendly."

When I became DDCI, I had some scars from previous mistakes as well as some painfully acquired experiences about what worked and what did not. Serving as a deputy in a number of different positions allowed me to learn by watching both the successes and failures of my bosses. Webster gave me a great deal of freedom to act independently, particularly in the area of intelligence analysis.

Bob Gates' experience as deputy to Bill Casey left a real mark on my thinking. Covert action involving Iran and the Contras had denied him his first effort to become the DCI. I decided early on that I was going to stick close to the Directorate of Operations, particularly in the area of sensitive operations or covert action. It was the area where most of the CIA's problems originated. The reason is obvious. The operations people were the action arm of the Agency and accidents, mistakes, or even successes often resulted in attacks by friends and foes alike. I became very familiar with most activities and programs and stayed with them from beginning to end. Because I was interested in these activities, as well as concerned about them from a risk viewpoint, I spent a great deal of time discussing these programs with their managers. In my view, this focus on clandestine activity paid off because I was able to respond to questions before they became problems. But there were times when even intense preparation did not help. Congressional oversight after the Iran-Contra affair was intrusive and burdensome.

My other priority as DDCI was to follow the key national security problems and help develop and present the analysis of the Intelligence Community. During this period, the CIA had excellent contacts with the policy maker. The President understood the limitations and value of intelligence. General Scowcroft was an experienced customer and Bob Gates probably was the best-prepared deputy national security adviser in history. Dick Cheney, the Secretary of Defense, had been an active member of the House Permanent Selection Committee for Intelligence and had a large and capable intelligence staff supporting him. Secretary of State James Baker was a very focused and critical customer. Other senior State and Defense officials—Bob Kimmitt, Paul Wolfowitz, Admiral Dave Jeremiah and most of the policy people in defense and state were outstanding. It was an extraordinary foreign policy team.

The Deputies Committee

Even before the inauguration in 1989, General Scowcroft and Bob Gates developed a new process for handling national security issues. A Deputies Committee was established to provide a forum for interagency consideration of national security issues. The members included Robert Kimmitt, the Undersecretary of State for Policy, Admiral Dave Jeremiah, the Vice Chairman of the Joint Chiefs of Staff, Paul Wolfowitz, Undersecretary of Defense for Policy and me. Other agency deputies were included depending on the subject under consideration. Bob Gates was the chairman of the group.

Never in my experience in the government has a group worked so well together and accomplished so much. While we all got tired of attending meetings, especially during crises, the group developed an easy relationship. The Deputies Committee probably was the high point of interagency cooperation. Many problems between the CIA and Defense and State were worked out during an informal chat at Deputy meetings. An important strength of the Deputies Committee was that when the group reached a decision, the members had sufficient authority that they could implement that decision in their organizations.

The Deputies Committee worked best when it was dealing with the more traditional national security policies. Panama, arms control, developments in the Soviet Union and East Europe, Afghanistan, North Korea, crisis in the Philippines, and the invasion of Kuwait by Iraq were grist for the mill. The traditional national security organizations knew how to deal with crises and difficult problems.

The process tended to break down a bit when organizations and agencies not normally involved in national security were added to the core group. Drug trafficking was a good example of this problem. Any Deputies meeting on drugs usually involved dozens of people, not the half-dozen principals that usually considered national security problems. This was good evidence that no one was in charge of this particular problem. Many of the people attending these meetings had no real authority in their organizations, so they could not implement decisions even if decisions had been made. Technology control and some economic issues were other examples when the process did not work particularly well. Arms control, a black art, was effectively handled by a separate group. Consequently, most arms control issues were settled before they got to the Deputies level.

The Reagan and Bush Administrations dealt with some of the most significant and diverse set of foreign policy issues since the Truman Administration. While many of these issues were set in motion during the Reagan Administration, it was his successor who faced the "velvet" revolution in East Europe, the reunification of Germany and fundamental change in the Soviet Union. For a CIA observer it is interesting that when Bush was the DCI, one of his major crises was the tree-cutting incident along the DMZ in Korea when a US non-commissioned officer was killed. How times had changed.

Going to the White House

When I was involved in the daily process of producing the President's Daily Brief, I went to the White House several times to meet with Richard Allen, the National Security Adviser. My first trip to the West Wing of the White House was a significant event. I was excited. That feeling of excitement never left even though I regularly went to Deputies meeting in the situation room. I usually arrived early for the meeting and on few times just wandered around the White House looking at picture and enjoying the experience.

The Deputies met in the windowless situation room located in the West Wing. A small room with large table surrounded by chairs along the walls. Somewhat claustrophobic but private.

Covering the World

Obviously, the Intelligence Community followed all national security issues and most countries. In addition, it tried to look ahead at problems that had not yet grabbed the policymaker's attention. During both the Reagan and Bush Administrations, the Soviet Union was the highest priority. The CIA and other agencies and departments had developed a strong group of analysts steeped in following the internal politics and external behavior of the Soviet Union and its Warsaw Pact allies. China was another country where the analytic expertise was deep and sophisticated.

While I represented the views of analysts working the

top-priority countries, I tended to focus much of my time on the "third world." This was the area where major crises arose with alarming regularity. As a result, I worked hard to get a working knowledge of places like Panama, South Africa, Iraq and Iran, Nicaragua, and Libya, as well as the terrorist and drug problems. As mentioned before, I also placed heavy emphasis on the areas where there were covert action programs. I figured that the Soviet and East European problems were well covered by a host of experts, and I could rely on them for sound analysis. There were strong analysts in other areas, but fewer of them, and the policymakers had less knowledge and experience working these somewhat "less" important problems. I thought I could be most useful to the policymakers if I developed some expertise in these areas.

Intelligence—that means "the CIA" to most—is often criticized for not predicting the future. Like most criticisms, there is a bit of truth in this observation. Most of those who try to look into the future tend to have straight line projections based on an assessment of what is currently happening. What we see now will get worse or become less of a problem, but it will retain its basic character regardless. There are good reasons why analysts have difficulty dealing with discontinuity. Continuity shaped by history and culture is the more likely outcome even in countries under great stress. History suggests that analysts who conclude that the glue holding a country together is stronger than the forces pulling it apart are right most of the time. The problem is that when they are wrong, they are really wrong and the implications for US policy are significant.

Early in the Bush Administration, there was a major

foreign policy review. Iraq was one of the countries focused on in this review. During the spring of 1989 there was a full-blown cabinet meeting on US policy toward Iraq. I went to that meeting for Webster because he was travelling. The analysts working Iraq had given me a well-prepared outline of what was happening in Iraq. Saddam Hussein had murdered opponents inside and outside Iraq and was ruthlessly suppressing his opposition inside the country. He had embarked upon an aggressive program to develop nuclear weapons and was illegally purchasing technology abroad. He also continued to build his conventional military forces far beyond any reasonable defensive need. The briefing I presented to the cabinet was pessimistic and ended with a statement that it was unlikely that "this leopard would change its spots." The administration decided to extend agricultural credits to Iraq despite its bad behavior.

Unfortunately, a national intelligence estimate done later that year was less clear about the danger from Iraq. Intelligence continued to monitor Iraq during the summer of 1990 but was distracted a bit because so much of Saddam's attention was focused on Israel.

The buildup along the Kuwait border was identified early on and the current intelligence publications described the situation with increasing concern. About two weeks before the invasion of Kuwait, the publications were reporting that it was likely that Iraqi forces would cross the border. Some analysts believed that the Iraqis would just invade northern Kuwait and occupy the oil fields. But there was little question that Iraq could overpower Kuwait easily.

Clarity about Iraqi intention was lacking in part because

the US Ambassador to Kuwait was convinced that there would not be an invasion and many of the Gulf nations agreed. At a Deputies meeting the day before the invasion, Bob Kimmitt who was chairing the meeting, asked me on a scale of 10 where I would put the probability of the Iraqi's invading Kuwait. I said I would give it a 9. Later that evening, I was talking with a group of reporters at a dinner. When they asked about the possibility of an invasion, it was difficult not to give them the same assessment.

The CIA support to the military and reporting on the effectiveness of economic sanctions against Saddam was excellent. Bill Webster did an excellent job of presenting the evidence and the conclusions on the effectiveness of the sanctions in an open congressional hearing, but he concluded that the sanctions alone would not cause Saddam to leave Kuwait. Unfortunately, the type of information the CIA had been developing on Iraq did not provide the detail necessary galvanize the US to prepare for military operations. That led to a lot of criticism of the CIA. This was unfair in my view, because the CIA was in the business of providing strategic intelligence for policymakers not detailed tactical information for operating forces. I believe there still is some confusion about the role the CIA should play when US forces are engaged.

One of the more interesting problems that arose during the war was the role of the CIA in assessing damage. The CIA historically had provided an independent assessment of the status and effectiveness of US military actions. But as it began to follow the war in Kuwait, there was considerable concern that the CIA's questioning some of the reporting on bomb damage would feed or create opposition to the war and open an unwanted and divisive debate. General Colin Powell was adamant that the CIA should not use information on US forces in its reporting. General Scowcroft was less than enthusiastic about reporting what damage was or was not being inflicted on the Iraqi forces because it often was different than reporting from the field.

So, what was the CIA's role? It had some of the most experienced photographic interpreters in the government. For example, they were truly experts on the Scud missile that presented such a political problem when fired against Israel. The CIA stopped counting "kills" of Scud missiles when reporting from the field reached 200. CIA photographic interpreters were not convinced that any Scud missiles or launchers had been destroyed as reported by the US military. They were right.

In my judgment, policymakers do need an independent capability to assess whether the military is achieving it objectives and the stated policy goals. This independent assessment probably was less essential during a quick and nearly painless war, but it would be important if the military action was drawn out over an extended period of time and there were significant casualties. No organization should write the report cards for its own programs.

One further observation on Iraq. Prior to the beginning of the air war, the Deputies Committee had regularly discussed the objectives of the war and the limits that should be set in fighting. While everyone knew that Saddam was the problem and hopefully would not survive the war or the defeat, they also knew how important the alliance was to the effort to drive Saddam's forces from Kuwait. The decision not to invade Iraq was a tough one because of the uncertainty of where that would leave Saddam after the war. In my view, it was a good decision. The administration had clearly outlined its goals and discussed the options, and then stuck to its policy.

In 1989, about six months after the student protests in Tiananmen Square, I went to China. I had some CIA business to conduct with the Chinese, but I also wanted to see how the country was reacting to the aftermath of the protests the previous May. My party included my wife, the heads of the Chinese units in the directorates of intelligence and operations, and staff and security.

Initially, others in the Agency suggested that I not travel with my wife on overseas trips. My general counsel advised against it. I countered by arguing that she was an asset to the Agency and me. When she traveled with me, I noticed that our hosts felt obliged to have their wives attend dinners. That meant a much looser talk around the table and also meant that Jan was invited to lunches where the women exchanged stories about what was going on from their point of view. She also was able to talk with secretaries in the CIA stations and get a good sense of what was happening. She became a valuable intelligence collector.

In China, the host of our visit was the head of Chinese military intelligence. In his late '60s or early '70s, he had been in the People's Liberation Army (PLA) for decades and the head of intelligence for many years.

At our first meeting, the Chinese and Americans sat on opposite sides of a long table with the heads of the delegation in the center. It was very formal, and the Director of Military Intelligence set the tone with a long speech about how the US had fomented the student unrest in Tiananmen. He said that the US had filled students' heads with propaganda and was responsible for their violence. He used several rather interesting illustrations such as, "The US had put the bell on the cow and now it was up to us to remove it." (I am sure there is a Chinese proverb that describes this picture.)

Soon it was my turn to respond and for about 15 minutes I said, in a variety of ways, that his claim of US responsibility for the student unrest was "bullshit." I cannot remember whether I asked one of my Agency linguists for the right words in Chinese. I said that the Chinese were well aware of the causes behind the student protests, and they all could be traced back to actions by their government. We ended this drama and got down to work on issues of concern to both countries.

There were a couple of incidents that provided some insight into Chinese culture. One morning, Jan and the wife of one of the station officers went shopping on their own to avoid Chinese escorts. That afternoon the Chinese official managing our visit told me that I needed to tell my wife she was not to go off by herself. I responded by saying that I did not tell my wife what to do in her free time.

The next day, the women had scheduled a shopping trip and wanted to leave at a specific time in the afternoon because they need to get ready for a formal dinner. Our hosts said it would be better to wait an hour or so. The ladies were certain about the time they wanted to leave and said so. The Chinese nodded in apparent agreement, but when they went to leave, the car had a flat tire and it was not fixed until the time the Chinese had specified.

At the end of the trip, the celebratory dinner was fascinating. Our host was Mao's doctor who had accompanied him on the "long march" and who was quite willing to talk about his adventures.

In Washington DC, Judge Webster got a call from Senator Hatch of Utah telling him that he had a person he would like to see appointed as a National Intelligence Officer at CIA. He wanted the Director to come to a meeting with him and Senator Humphrey from New Hampshire to discuss the issue. The Judge decided that I should go to the meeting, and it was set up with the Senator.

On the day of the appointment I was escorted up into the attic of the Capitol where Senator Humphrey had his office. It was the most unusual office I had ever been in. In this dark, crowded, cranny filled with books and odd furniture, Senator Hatch, Senator Humphrey and Michael Pillsbury greeted me. This felt more like a trial than a social call. Senator Hatch took the lead and proceeded to describe the qualifications of Michael Pillsbury. I knew a good deal about Pillsbury and guessed what was coming, but just sat there and listened.

Michael Pillsbury, a scion of the flour company, was well known in the Intelligence Community and had worked for the Defense Department and as a foreign policy adviser to several senators. He was an expert on China, fluent in the language, and very outspoken. He also was considered an ideologue with strongly held views. He definitely was not a team player. He had been accused of unauthorized release of some classified information, and his clearances had been lifted by the Defense Department.

Even though I knew what was coming, it took some time to get to the point. Senator Hatch wanted Pillsbury appointed as a senior officer in CIA. To be specific, he wanted him to be what was known as a National Intelligence Officer—the lead officer of a specific geographic area who led work on national estimates and spoke for the Director of Central Intelligence.

What followed was a little embarrassing for Pillsbury, or at least it should have been. He was sitting right next to me as l described why I would not put him in the job as NIO. I was quite blunt in stating why I could not agree to their request. Pillsbury was a person who could not approach the China problem as a team player, listening to others and representing their views. He was an expert but was also known as someone who leaked information when he disagreed with policy. He was not someone who could be given a senior position in the Intelligence Community, a position where he would influence the key products that were intended to provide objective analysis fairly representing the different points of view to policymakers. My organization would think I had lost my mind or at a minimum, caved to political pressure.

The senators pushed back and said that Pillsbury offered some needed expertise and contrary views to an organization that had often been proven to be wrong on key issues and needed new blood. I disagreed and said that contrary views were useful but not those from someone who already had his mind made up regardless of the evidence. They asked me to reconsider my decision, and the meeting was over. I was sweating when I left that cold room, and I realized that Pillsbury never said a word during this 30-minute discussion.

It was clear when I left the meeting that this problem was not going away. I reported back to the Director, who was a bit uncomfortable about turning down a request from Senator Hatch. A few days later I got a call from Senator Hatch asking me if I had reconsidered their proposal. I said I had thought about it but had not changed my mind. He spent several minutes trying to convince me and said he would call back in a few days. He did. Several days later he called again and asked the same question but added that I should remember that he was a senior member of my oversight committee and might well end up as chairman in the near future. At the end of my patience, I said that I was not going to change my mind and thought his calls were aimed at bullying me to do something that I thought was wrong. I did not hear from the Senator again.

Throughout this drama, I thought of myself as the lead character in *Mr. Smith Goes to Washington*; standing up to outside forces and sticking to principle. The problem was clearly explained to me a bit later in a discussion with a former congressman who said what I had experienced was commonplace on the Hill. Congressmen frequently asked others for help on a bill or with constituents even though they may not agree on the issue, but with the understanding that the favor would be repaid in the future. You scratch my back, and I will scratch yours. I had not played the game.

In hindsight, I could have been more creative and offered Pillsbury a job as a consultant who would offer a different perspective on our analysis thus helping out the senators and giving CIA the benefit of an alternative view. I could have figured out a way to explain my actions to a skeptical organization and gained two important supporters on the Hill. Nevertheless, I remain convinced that my stand on Pillsbury was the right one. Who knows, maybe the senators appreciated someone who stuck to principle.

I will admit being impressed by the 2016 book *The Hundred-Year Marathon* that Pillsbury wrote about China, though it did not change my mind that he was not a good fit as a National Intelligence Officer.

6.

ACTING DIRECTOR OF CENTRAL INTELLIGENCE

I became the Acting Director of Central Intelligence in September 1991 after Bill Webster retired and while Bob Gates was in the confirmation process. The two-month period until Bob Gates was sworn in was a busy one. Events don't wait for personnel changes.

During this period, there were a lot of interesting things to keep my attention. One experience clearly illustrated the kind of pressures placed on a DCI, or in this case, an Acting DCI. The CIA had been accused of working with the Bank of Credit and Commerce International (BCCI), a bank registered in Luxembourg with offices in Karachi and London. The BCCI had been the cause of concern during the 1980s because it was poorly regulated and subsequently found to be involved in various financial crimes.

In particular, the CIA was criticized for not informing the appropriate US authorities that the BCCI had bought a US bank. CIA had informed the Department of Treasury about the transaction, but that did not quell the criticism. This problem finally led to a public hearing before a Congressional committee looking into the full range of BCCI activities. It was one of my rare public hearings, and I participated only under duress.

The hearing was primarily for public consumption with a lot of posturing by the two congressional participants, particularly Senator John Kerry. Another senator wanted me to identify the person who did not send the Federal Reserve the information on the purchase of the US bank by BCCI. I responded that the Federal Reserve was not a normal recipient of classified intelligence, and I would not give the names of CIA people involved. American journalist Mary McGrory was outraged that I would not tell the senators the name of the individual responsible for deciding what dissemination the report received. I said I would take the responsibility because I believed the right choices had been made. She said that statement "exhibited an unfamiliarity with the repentance curve." She indicated that the exchange with the senators "illustrated the difficulty of reconciling a secret intelligence agency with democratic openness." She was partially right. It did demonstrate the problem of open public hearings held for political purposes on subjects involving sensitive sources and methods. The day after the hearing, an article about the proceedings titled "BCCI: Politics and Politesse" by Mary McGrory was published in *The Washington Post*.

Before I became Acting Director, there was a growing problem that I did not appreciate. The Agency had been trying to get some new facilities for handling equipment and supplies. The area of Cameron Station in Alexandria was the primary depot. At the same time, there was consideration about getting some of our support personnel out of the Washington area because of the cost to employees. The Agency began looking at alternative areas and someone came up with the idea of West Virginia. A study of land, living costs and transportation suggested that West Virginia might be an ideal location. A surprising number of employees lived in the state or along the Virginia border and commuted. The Agency began looking at specific locations and found some land that was well situated and reasonably priced.

It was about this time in the process that I was briefed on the project. It made a good deal of sense—move to an area where living costs were lower, land was available at good price, and the functions involved were improved by new facilities without affecting operational support.

My reaction to the proposal was to be supportive, but the entire project suffered from one critical problem: it was a political folly. Several things happened to make it so. Most importantly, we did not take into account the political impact of moving local workers out of the state. We did not prepare the groundwork with our oversight committees, and we did not anticipate the reaction of local politicians. We had not prepared anyone for change.

A major storm erupted. First, Senator Byrd of West Virginia got wind of our plans and became a major advocate. Sometimes you can have supporters who are a real liability. Second, Congressman Wolfe of Northern Virginia seriously opposed moving some CIA personnel and operations out of his district. Third, our oversight committees decided that this move was another maneuver by Senator Byrd to add government facilities to the growing number already in West Virginia.

Congressman Wolfe made an appointment to talk with me about the proposed moved of facilities and personnel to West Virginia. It was the most unusual conversation. He said that this moment was an opportunity for me to "choose the high road like in the movie *Mr. Smith Goes to Washington* and act on principle." I should turn down Senator Byrd's proposal. Congressman Wolfe spent considerable time talking about Mr. Smith's courage and why I should follow his example. I was amused by his reference to a movie that I often felt mirrored by my own experiences, but I had to stay on topic. I was baffled and said so. We were doing what seemed best for the organization and its personnel. The reduced cost was clear and the advantage to personnel sound. He kept returning to the movie theme until he finally left, unsatisfied.

The full irritation of our oversight committees and the opposition by Congressman Wolfe came just as I was about to leave the CIA and Bob Gates was to be the Director. He had to pull the Agency from the project and Senator Byrd became so irritated that he cut some money from the CIA's operating budget.

When President Bush nominated Bob Gates as Director of Central Intelligence, it was clear I would have to retire. General Scowcroft and Gates had come to the conclusion that a ranking military officer was needed as Deputy. The Director of NSA, Vice Admiral William Studeman, was selected as DDCI and given a fourth star.

I was unhappy at leaving so abruptly and because of events outside my control. Nevertheless, there was a great send off with parties and ceremony. Most important, there was a genuine expression of affection and respect from the working analysts and managers in the agency. You cannot ask for more than that.

I decided that I would do something a bit different on my last morning trip to CIA headquarters. I told my driver, George Patrick, to get in the backseat of my 1948 black Oldsmobile, and I dove him to the building followed by my limo and chaser car. I thought it a fitting ending and there hanging down the front of the building were sheets with "goodbye Dick" and "we will miss you" written on them.

I was given a grand send off with an early evening gathering of well over 100 guests at the CIA. Several of my early bosses including Dick Helms, Ray Cline, Dick Lehman, and Ed Motsinger were there as were Bill Webster and Bob Gates. Mrs. William Casey and her family, a senior congressional staffer, Richard Haas and Admiral Dave Jerimiah attended as well. The turnout of senior CIA officers and staff was particularly heartwarming. Even a number of neighbors and Great Falls friends were in attendance, and few had ever been inside CIA before. My retirement party turned into a bit of a roast with two of the staff wearing the "Big Bird" and "gorilla" costumes Jan had made for my Halloween parties.

I was offered a couple of jobs in the administration but declined. I was still working on getting an ambassadorial position when the Bush Administration ended in 1992. For a few months, I took time to just catch my breath. But after being involved in the key issues of the moment for 30 years, it was not easy to come to a full stop. Golf and tennis were not adequate substitutes for involvement with interesting problems and committed people. Few things can beat being involved with a group of bright people trying to understand a complex national security problem.

During my career I worked for the following CIA Directors:

- Allen Welsh Dulles   Eisenhower
- John Alexander McCone   Kennedy
- William Francis Raborn   Johnson
- Richard McGarrah Helms   Johnson
- James Rodney Schlesinger   Nixon
- William Egan Colby   Nixon
- George Herbert Walker Bush Ford
- Stansfield Turner   Carter
- William Hedgcock Webster   Reagan
- Robert Michael Gates   Bush

7.

COLLEAGUES

Those in the corporate world have heard of 360-degree feedback. Basically, it's the idea that bosses/supervisors review their employees as expected, but the employees and even other coworkers also get a chance to write a review about their bosses. It's intended to give a complete, holistic view of the working relationship from all involved parties. I'm not sure how beneficial it is, but along those same lines, I invited some of my colleagues, employees, and friends to give their thoughts on our adventures in the CIA.

Parker "Chip" Schofield

I asked the Director of Operations to select an experienced officer to serve as a special assistant as soon as I was selected as Deputy Director. Parker "Chip" Schofield was their choice. And a good one. He had served in Europe and Asia, was a linguist, and a truly competent and amusing person.

On a sultry August afternoon in 1990, a Deputies Meeting was hurriedly convened to address an urgent foreign affairs issue. Due to severe time constraints, the meeting was conducted via teleconferencing rather than in person in the situation room of the White House. The Deputy Director of the Central Intelligence Agency, Richard James Kerr, was charged with providing intelligence and risk assessments to the assembled Deputy Agency Directors and Deputy Department Secretaries. At the appointed hour, Mr. Kerr strode into the teleconference center at CIA headquarters and began his presentation. He was wearing a blue suit, tie, and plastic Groucho Marx glasses, nose and mustache. Not a single participant mentioned the getup. They knew with whom they were dealing.

Such is Dick Kerr—a smart man, and whimsical. Dick's adventurous and lighter side are always near the surface. On Halloween he prowled the hallways of Langley (CIA Headquarters) in a full gorilla suit. Occasionally when working late on a Spring or Autumn evening and the seventh-floor hallways and offices empty, Dick would magically produce a bottle of wine, push a couple of chairs out the window of his office and invite his staff to vespers on the roof.

Dick's knowledge of the CIA was comprehensive. It is safe to say that none of his predecessors or successors as Deputy or Acting Director knew the nooks and crannies of the CIA as Dick did. Some were outsiders—military officers, politicians, or judges. Others were career CIA officers, but had come up through the ranks in only one of the four Directorates—usually Intelligence or Operations. Not so Dick Kerr. He began life in the CIA as a lowly GS-7 analyst/clerk. He rose rapidly through the bureaucracy, serving in all four directorates (Intelligence, Operations, Administration, and Science and Technology) and reaching Director level in both Intelligence and Administration before becoming DDCI.

Dick Kerr is a man about whom I have never heard an ill word spoken. On his retirement in March 1992 officers from all four directorates donated sheets which were hung from the roof of the entire front of CIA headquarters with the simple message "We will miss you Dick!" This was a gesture unprecedented in CIA history.

Aris Pappas

I asked Aris Pappas to join the Kerr Group examining the intelligence leading up to the war with Iraq because I considered him one of the most experienced and creative Soviet analysts. He had served as an Assistant National Intelligence Officer working on Soviet ground forces, had served on rotation at the FBI, attended the US Navy War College, and taught a course on "Intelligence and War" at Johns Hopkins University.

Shortly after retiring from the CIA in 2003, I was invited by former Deputy Director Dick Kerr to join a small group he was putting together to do a special study related to the decision to attack Iraq. Months before the actual conflict, Secretary of Defense Donald Rumsfeld, had requested that the Agency prepare an unusual assessment.

Rumsfeld wanted a review of all the intelligence material that was being provided to the most senior decision-makers in support of the decision to attack Iraq. The study group was then to await the outcome of the impending conflict, reassemble, and compare the many estimates, assessments, Presidential Daily Briefings, and other finished intelligence with the "ground truth" that was expected to be uncovered. Director George Tenet, called in Mr. Kerr to perform this unprecedented task. He was going to write a report card for the Intelligence Community.

We were provided a large room into which the Agency placed shelves and computers containing all the pertinent material. Dick assigned each of us to a specific issue. One was to review material related to Iraq generically; another was to review material related to the nexus between Iraq and established terrorist groups, especially al-Qaida; and I was to review material assessing Iraq's military capabilities and intentions.

We each dove into the material with enthusiasm. None of us had seen these particular products and judgments before but were eager to read them. If what we'd all seen and read in public sources was correct, then the classified material should be that much more compelling. It was not to be.

The first document I read was the now infamous Weapons of Mass Destruction Estimate. Like the al-Qaida relationship, the WMD issue was a principal driver of US decisions, so I was anxious to see what the Intelligence Community had to say. I can still remember my reaction to what I read. Dick was sitting in the office when I approached him with the Estimate and said something like "this is a bag of air." Having read it himself earlier, he simply smiled at me and said, "I know." I repeated my comment with some more emphasis, and he repeated his response. As the days went by, we discovered more and more serious flaws in collection, analysis, and production.

The WMD Estimate had been written by three different National Intelligence Officers, one each for the Chemical, Biological, and Nuclear sections. These three issues, though related, were not identical in terms of Iraq's assessed intentions or capabilities. Each NIO, moreover, had his own individual approach to his problem, to include the use of evidence and analysis. Produced on a very short schedule, the Estimate and other products suffered from a lack of substantive editing and management review that might otherwise have caught their most egregious problems.

Intelligence officers are often faced with situations in which the available evidence is inadequate to support a firm judgment. For this reason, intelligence assessments are supposed to contain mandatory sections that outline their underlying assumptions; highlight alternative conclusions; and, identify gaps in the available intelligence. The WMD Estimate contained none of these basic elements.

The others were running into similar problems with the material they were reviewing. One, for example, could not find credible intelligence to support the contention that Saddam was directly supporting al-Qaida. Another found many pertinent and accurate reports, but there was a failure to consolidate and integrate their findings into a coherent picture of Saddam's Iraq.

As a result of these problems, the idea of disbanding us in anticipation of ground truth was given up and we began immediately to look into how and why these basic, and frankly inexcusable, problems had occurred. The Agency's initial reaction was, perhaps understandably, defensive. We were asked to take a closer look at the issue and were even provided access to the primary source material that informed some of the judgments. Dick was not eager to prepare a second report, saying that the results would not differ. Indeed, they did not.

What we found was a systemic breakdown in analysis and presentation. Almost every aspect of the process was broken or ignored. Inadequate collection resulted in reliance on dated or questionable reporting. That, in turn, was exacerbated by a failure to clearly identify where conclusions were solidly supported by evidence and where they were analytical constructs dependent on unchallenged and unstated assumptions. We completed two classified studies, followed by an unclassified version, "Intelligence and Analysis on Iraq: Issues for the Intelligence Community," that was made available to the public on 29 July 2004. Tom Wolfe and I also appeared on Maria Bartiromo's TV program to discuss the study in some length. The conclusion was that Intelligence had "ultimately failed in its singular mission to accurately inform policy deliberations."

There was a growing public and political belief that blame could be placed at the feet of Administration officials attempting to influence intelligence judgments to support evolving policy decisions or that individuals within the Intelligence Community had doctored the judgments. We could find no evidence of such actions. Had we found such evidence, it would have been a blessing because the solution would have been immediately available and instantly effective.

Instead we found a much more dangerous and difficult problem to address. Its roots were set in the failure of the Intelligence Community to protect its basic standards and practices. Such process problems are pervasive, require strong and dedicated management effort, and can take over a generation to resolve.

It's difficult to imagine anyone but Dick being able to direct our effort and help us navigate past the many hot-button items that presented themselves. His stabilizing influence served to guide us as we examined the material, while his reputation for integrity and objectivity was the unique key to our ability to present our unappealing findings. His conclusion read:

"US intelligence is a robust, highly capable, and thoroughly motivated community that represents an invaluable asset to the nation and its citizens. It must reveal itself as sufficiently mature to both adapt to changing circumstances and counteract evolutionary processes that have conspired to threaten its reputation and its ability to successfully perform its assigned mission. The alternative is unacceptable and unthinkable."

John G. D. Grieve

Professor John Grieve was a former Deputy Assistant Commissioner in the Metropolitan Police. He is considered one of the most distinguished police leaders of his generation. John and I served on the Independent Monitoring Commission overseeing compliance with the Good Friday Agreement in Northern Ireland for seven years.

"No plaudits please," Dick told me. This account of my learning from him is intended to be an accurate record of his efforts in the peace process in Northern Ireland. It reflects my view of his contributions. These were never acknowledged by an ungrateful later British government. I have used it as a chance to revisit those great days I spent with Dick and so many others and to record what I learnt.

I first met Dick Kerr at a counter-terrorist intelligence conference at a stately home in the home counties of England in 1995. I made a mind map record of his fascinating counter terrorism intelligence analysis presentation of his over three decades of experiences. I have it in front of me as I write. I little thought that a decade and a half later I would be staying at his house and spending days in his company. Dick was a lifetime US Central Intelligence Agency analyst, a former head and a thoughtful commentator of intelligence gathering, analysis and assessment, both the theory and practice. I learnt a lot that first day.

Some years later, via the then Her Majesty's Chief Inspector of Constabulary (HMCIC), Jonathan Powell the Chief of Staff of the then British Prime Minister Tony Blair, sent for me. That was in 2004 two years after I had retired after nearly four decades of policing. He asked if I would accept a post as one of four Commissioners to monitor certain aspects of the Northern Ireland peace process following the Good Friday Agreement. Unbeknownst to me, a number of people had turned the task down as too difficult, if not impossible, due to the complexity of the Irish peace process. Justifying our title as an International Independent Monitoring Commission two other Commissioners were to be Joe Brosnan from the Department of Justice in Dublin and Dick Kerr. That and the fourth Commissioner was a politician and member of the House of Lords, John Alderdice.

Our work was based on an International Agreement between Dublin and London on 25th November 2003 and implemented by the Northern Ireland (Monitoring Commission etc.) Act 2003, Our objectives set out in Article 3 of the agreement were to promote the transition to a peaceful, stable and inclusive society and government in NI.

We had no chair, when we needed one, we took it in turns. The four Commissioners had equal status. At our first meetings, we roughed out our intentions practically and theoretically in a series of Principles and Guidelines. Our task was to ensure the paramilitaries went out of business; primacy given to ethical political leadership and the observance of duties and human rights. This applied equally to us and to others engaged with the paramilitaries. We would follow the evidence we collected where it led. We were not to be concerned with the destruction or putting beyond use of the vast stocks of weaponry the paramilitaries still held, that task was given to another international commission. We were to report on their behavior and the steps they took in support of the peace process and the transition required by the agreement and legislation.

A major issue for us, based on the legislation, was to be the confidentiality and protection of our sources and not to put any of them at risk. This included not just individuals but also national security. We strictly followed this in view of the contemporary continuing violent environment. Many unsuccessful attempts were made by lawyers, coroners, political parties, and individuals to get at the material behind our published reports.

We would seek corroboration of the information we received and in my case consilience (in the sense of different disciplines and institutions indicating similar conclusions and recommendations). We would describe the level of confidence we felt about the decisions we reached. We would meet as many people with as many and varied opinions as possible. We published our methodology and clarified our role on 9 March 2004.

We would produce a report every four months indicating where change for the better had been observed or the contrary. We would keep a detailed record of our processes, we would be accountable and where possible transparent (within the strict security limitations imposed by our *mandate to protect others in a still risky, potentially violent, post conflict or at least transitioning environment). We would have offices and regular meetings in Belfast and Dublin, some meetings in London and latterly in the US—Washington, New York, Boston and the Outer Banks of North Carolina. Our Dublin Office was given to us by the Taoiseach Bertie Aherne it was in Dublin Castle and in the actual former British intelligence offices that Michael Collins had burgled in 1919.*

We took it in turns as Commissioners to chair a Press Conference to release each of our reports and answer questions. This emphasized our transparency and accountability, we also had a web site and made ourselves available for many media interviews and public meetings with community groups from all parts of the Irish political spectrum.

We soon learnt how to use the synergy created by the diversity of the team and developed a highly creative process. This involved our hugely effective joint secretary Stephen Boys Smith preparing an initial draft for each of the 26 reports based on who we had met and what we had read, these then went through multiple iterations as each line was analyzed and every word explored, disagreements ironed out or explained. The reports were then slept on and explored over and over again. In the meantime, our ideas were thrashed out again over meals and during Hotel's happy hours.

Dick Kerr's intelligence experiences went back to the Bay of Pigs and John F. Kennedy. He had talked with every type of player on the world stage from Russians to the Taliban, with Presidents and peasants, with terrorist and torturers, with patriots and parsimonious self-serving cynics.

All this gave Dick a deep understanding not just of

intelligence as a discipline but also of people, of the human condition, of politics and diplomacy generally, specifically of extreme politics, of extremely violent ideologies, of allies and enemies. He learnt Russian and for years analyzed the global reach of Russia particularly the Soviet Navy. In a chapter for a book I edited, he called them "The Perfect Enemy." In Ireland, we were dealing with intelligence during a transition into a peace process, a society in a post conflict phase; so those former combatants we were talking to could hardly ever be described as an "enemy" perfect or otherwise. They were not even friends or allies in the process sometimes.

Dick's perspective and references to other conflicts was not just American but global and his quoted examples telling. He could examine the apparently unique nature of the Irish dilemmas from an Irish American perspective and then apply an explanation from something he had learnt elsewhere on the globe.

One of Dick's analytic tools explored how to get leverage on an issue. It was one his contributions to my thinking the use of intelligence led leverage on what might be seen otherwise as an intractable problem. He gave much though on how that leverage might be obtained.

His global reputation was huge and the Americans (the State Department, individuals Presidential and advisers, National Security Adviser, Congress, Senate, business, media and community groups) were major players in the peace process as were the CIA and FBI. Dick got us access into a wide range of interested, concerned, critical, supportive and useful parties. Not least Irish American significant players such as the US Northern Irish High Commissioner and Senator Mitchell the major architect of the peace process himself.

To my mind one of the more important openings he created for us was with a very rich US caucus of Irish supporters and their security advisers with Sinn Fein.

Dick is a big man both physically and psychologically, with the strong opinions of his Scottish emigrant forebears. This is tempered however with his capacity for review, for adaptation and reconsideration of the important issues when presented with other views, interpretation, assessment or ways of explaining/recording the point at issue. Widely read and a student of geography, history and archaeology he was fascinated by ideas but also by people. I heard him say on a number of occasions to terrorists, retired and otherwise, "I am just a simple American, I do not understand what you were saying," if you believed that then you were in trouble and I would listen to Dick unpack the illogicality and indeed the emotion in their arguments.

[When traveling] we were both early risers, first into breakfast, where Dick would discuss the day's world news and offer accounts of its origins, context, security implications and a role for intelligence. This became a sort of intellectual gym preparing me for the day's work.

At the other end of the day we would have a wider gathering. We were a sociable group and after each day's work we would have a debrief during the hotel happy hour, talking through the people we had met, what we had read and what it all might mean.

With such a sociable travelling group you would expect us to share other ideas and reading, this was wide-ranging from the relevant such as Margaret MacMillan's magisterial The Peace Makers *about the Versailles Conference at the end of World War One to what the Americans call "mysteries and thrillers" and we call "who-dun-its." I built up a library not just of Irish history and conflict commentary but also American political and security officials' biographies and security studies including works on the CIA and National Security Advisers.*

We also shared our taste in wine. The books and wine we paid for by ourselves and despite its relevance to our processes we did not claim for them. Dick was witty commentator, a raconteur and brilliant at telling jokes and self-deprecating anecdotes with great humor.

Susan D. Shiff

Sue Shiff worked as my assistant in the front office of the Directorate of Intelligence and came with me when I became the Deputy Director. She was the senior professional secretary in CIA and set the standards for performance.

I've known Dick Kerr for many years. When I first started working for him in 1985, he was the Associate Deputy Director for Intelligence and Robert Gates was the Director for Intelligence. Those first weeks working in the front office of the Directorate of Intelligence were a bit daunting to me. I kept thinking that Dick's decision to hire me as his Special Assistant must have been a leap of faith on his part, and he must have seen something in me that I had yet to recognize.

I soon realized that I couldn't have asked for a better "boss." We not only became great working partners, we became wonderful friends. And as I got to know Dick better in those early years, I learned he was not only very intelligent, and serious about his job, but, on the personal side, he had a great sense of humor, and was a wonderful family man. As the years went on, his wife, Jan, and I used to joke about me being Dick's "day wife." After all, we were together at least 12 hours a day at work.

My seven-year stint as Dick's "day-wife" encompassed four years in the Directorate of Intelligence, followed by three years as his Special Assistant when he became the Deputy Director of Central Intelligence (DDCI), and a period of time when he was Acting Director of Central Intelligence.

Working with Dick in the Intelligence Directorate and in the DDCI office, was always busy and challenging, but also a perfect opportunity to learn the history of our allies—and our enemies. Dick was a great teacher, and his insight and analysis of world situations was amazing.

Although we worked long hours, Dick always knew how to relieve the stress. Occasionally we would have a "crazy hat day," and we would liven things up at Halloween when the whole office would wear costumes. Some years we had a theme, and the rest of the time we "winged" it.

Our workday was unrelenting and jam-packed with meetings—both at CIA and the Intelligence Community meetings held at the White House. I also traveled to many foreign countries where Dick met with foreign dignitaries. Joining us on our trips were intelligence analysts, operations analysts, security personnel, and his real wife. Dick's intelligence, insight and warm personality were evident in every situation. Without hesitation I can honestly say that my seven years working with Richard J. Kerr were the highlight of my 35-year career with the Central Intelligence Agency. He welcomed me into his family, treated me as an integral part of his team, taught me that a bit of humor was a good antidote to stress and long hours. My friendship with both Dick and Jan now spans 34 years. I have so many wonderful memories of our association and the work we *accomplished on behalf of our great country. I will forever cherish our time together and be thankful that he selected me to join him on his journey at CIA.*

8.

TRAVEL, TRAVEL, TRAVEL

I managed to see much of the world over my thirty years with the CIA and several working trips after retirement. One of the most interesting and valuable learning experiences was a trip to Africa in 1990. The party included the chief of Africa Division, Bill Mosby, my special assistant, my wife and security and administrative support. We started in Uganda, went south to Zimbabwe, then to South Africa, Zambia, and Senegal. For someone very interested in Africa, the trip was exciting and eye-opening.

Uganda had been rid of Idi Amin—known as the butcher of Uganda for his brutality—for only a few years. The current president, a fairly enlightened former military officer, remains in power. Many of those in government positions had fled into the jungle to escape the wrath of Idi Amin. It was an impressive group, well educated at English universities. I had a good opportunity to exchange views about developments in Africa and talk about the leadership hopes for Uganda. Clearly, the President intended to play a role in African affairs, not just Uganda.

There was still considerable concern about tribal unrest in the country. Security was very intense and during a dinner at the home of a senior official shots were fired outside. Jan and I followed the example as all the diners got under the table.

From Uganda, the party flew south to Zimbabwe. I was not particularly welcomed by President Mugabe but was well received by intelligence and defense officials. The Deputy Head of Intelligence had put his current boss in jail during the fight for independence, but relations between the two seemed fine. In fact, the Deputy has just been given a national performance award. The government was good enough to offer a few days at safari camps and gave us a great tour of Victoria Falls. Zimbabwe was a beautiful, rich country but even then, it was clearly suffering economically.

A primary objective of the trip was to visit South Africa and get a better sense of what was happening there. The year 1990 was momentous in South Africa as dramatic change was underway. The President of South Africa, F. W. de Klerk had announced moves toward ending apartheid and starting universal suffrage. In 1990 the President ended the South African nuclear weapons program and had his first meeting with Nelson Mandela. In meetings with South African officials, intelligence and military, you could sense the winds of change and considerable apprehension about the future. They knew the end of white domination was near.

Jan had some interesting conversations with the wives of senior officials over lunch and dinner. Probably more than many people, they understood what the changes meant to them personally.

Twenty years after that trip to South Africa, I returned, but this time the visit was as a board member of a company that owned two small companies there. There were some management issues with these units, and I was sent to work out the problems.

In the intervening years between trips, I had done significant reading about South Africa and become particularly interested in Jan Smuts, a South African general in WWI and WWII, prime minister, and one of the principal creators of the League of Nations. While in Johannesburg, I asked my host if he could take me to the Smuts House Museum. It was very interesting with a large, simple house on 53 acres, a huge library, and a limo parked in front. All a bit run down. I was the only visitor. In talking to the staff, I found out that there was little interest in Smuts and no mention of him in current school history books. History started with the end of apartheid.

After the drama of South Africa, the visit to Zambia seemed calm. We got a short tour outside the capital and saw some native villages that looked like pictures from the past. We had a black crew member from the plane with us, and he made this revealing statement: "Looking at these villages and how primitive and poor the people are makes me glad my ancestors were taken as slaves to the United States."

The discussions with the President of Zambia, Kenneth Kaunda, were very interesting. He had been a leader of the revolutionary movement in Africa and had been President since the country became independent. He said he was not going to run for President again and generally was very pessimistic about the future of South Africa.

Our last stop was Senegal. I had an opportunity to visit the port where many blacks were shipped off to the new world. It was very depressing. My discussions with the President of Senegal were useful; he was preparing to make an official visit to the US and wanted to talk about US–African relations.

When the President of Senegal visited the US and a State dinner was organized, I asked my secretary to get an invitation for Jan and me and Bill Mosby and his wife to attend. She apparently got a very negative response, so I asked her to call again and say that I had just returned from a visit to Senegal and had told the President I would see him at dinner in Washington. Still not a yes. So, I told her to say that I would call President Bush. We got the invitation; Jan was seated at the front table. I was placed in the back as far away as possible.

In January 1993, a Pakistani terrorist killed two and wounded three CIA employees as they sat in their cars at a red light waiting to enter the CIA headquarters in Langley, Virginia.

One of the victims was Nickolas Starr, a close friend. He was badly wounded in the left shoulder as the terrorist fired through the window of his car. Jan and I went to the hospital in Fairfax that evening to visit with Nick's wife, Joy. She was worried about returning home because the shooter had not been caught. I called the CIA security and asked them to send officers to the hospital and the Starr's home. The assassin was hunted down in Pakistan and returned to the US where he was tried and executed.

CIA Changes Over the Years

When I joined the Agency in 1960, it was populated by former OSS officers, a number of well-educated graduates from the Ivy League and retirees from the US military. The major action in the Agency was overseas, led by the clandestine service, the Directorate of Operations. CIA chiefs of station were often the face of the Agency and in some countries, they carried more weight than the ambassadors. There were some impressive leaders in the early days of the Directorate of Intelligence, primarily in the Office of Current Intelligence. Many in the leadership were members of the Washington elite and fit in with other well-connected players on the political and diplomatic scene.

The composition of CIA personnel began to change as it became a force in new intelligence collection technology. The program offices that managed the development of the U-2, SR-71, and imagery and signals satellites, and exploited the information collected required a different sort of analyst and the technical expertise. Analysts needed to learn how to analyze and report of the flood of new technical information that was being acquired. The Directorate of Science and Technology became a key driver of the budget and product of CIA. New scientific and technical offices were created and manned by personnel from the national laboratories and missile test facilities.

More and more experienced analysts from the Directorate of Intelligence were being placed in key positions throughout the Agency, positions previously held by officers from the clandestine service. Many of these positions were held by officers trained by Bruce

Clarke. The Office of Strategic Research had a major impact on the management of CIA. But the entire organization was becoming more balanced with Directorate of Operations officers heading analytic offices and some analysts moving into overseas positions.

In the early days of the Agency the position of Deputy Director had filled by a military officer or an officer from the clandestine service. Bob Gates was only the second person from the analytic corps to move into that position and the first to become the Director of CIA. I was the third analyst to become a Deputy Director.

***

In my opinion, the best job in the US government was that of Deputy Director of CIA. I regularly told people that was the case. When I had the job, I had major responsibility for managing intelligence collection and analysis. As a member of the Deputies Committee, I had a significant role in policy formulation. In my role as Deputy Director Central Intelligence (one outside the role involving the Agency), I had some impact on the budget and policy of the other intelligence Agencies. At the same time, I was a bit sheltered from the political churn that the Director of CIA faced. William Webster took the brunt of that.

9.

CIA ASSESSMENT

It is a useful exercise to assess the strengths and weaknesses of a career. It probably can only be done after being separated from the business of intelligence for some reasonable period of time. I had some excellent job experiences and a variety of great teachers during more than three decades in the CIA. I had worked as an analyst, a manager of analysts, a manager of large organizations, and as a staffer. I had been involved in technical collection and policy issues that addressed the authorities of the Director of Central Intelligence. I grew to understand how fragile these authorities were and how easily they could be given away, particularly to an aggressive and capable Department of Defense. I had been involved in many of the major national security crises between 1962 and 1992. While I did not have deep expertise in any one area, I knew enough to place events in some historical context and to ask the key questions. I also learned that one attribute for a good intelligence officer was to assume you did not know all the answers and rely on those around you who were experts.

It also was important to have a certain amount of courage and be able to stand up to criticism and stick to your guns when senior policy officials called to complain that the intelligence publications, particularly briefings to Congress, were undermining policy. My response to one call from a senior official inside the White House who accused me of not supporting the "President's policy" was to say that the best support I could provide the President was an unvarnished presentation of the facts and clear analysis of the implications of those facts. It was important to be independent, but equally important to help the policymakers find opportunities as well as hear constructive criticism of their policy.

The CIA and the Intelligence Community had some impressive analysts with a real command of the subject matter. The key to success for any manager was to know who these stars were. It was equally important to know who was less capable, more manipulative, or inclined to turn analysis into policy recommendations. I spent most of my life as an analyst or managing analysts, so I knew many of the people in the DDI. I also spent a great deal of time discussing current and future issues with small groups of experts. Some of my most enjoyable times were spent in these sessions.

Some argued that I did not spend enough time on the management issues facing the CIA and the Intelligence Community. That was a legitimate complaint, but with limited time I believed that managing the organization really meant directing its intelligence production and staying involved with major collection activities. I probably spent too much time working on substantive issues, but that preparation served me well in the Deputies meetings. I found that preparing well for these meetings meant I could focus on two or three key issues and keep my briefings short and to the point. In my opinion, this approach was superior to reading a briefing paper prepared by others without my direct involvement. It was important to have enough knowledge about an issue to be able to match the intelligence input to the fast pace and diverse interests of the other participants.

The push-and-pull relationships between analysts and their managers was often upsetting to those who had not grown up inside the agency. A senior military officer assigned to the National Intelligence Council once expressed dismay at the constant arguing among analysts and was even more concerned that analysts would regularly argue with their bosses. There was little respect for rank other than some fear of Bob Gates. I engendered no such fear. It was not unusual for analysts to pop into my office and tell me that I had gotten this or that problem so screwed up nobody could straighten it out. Sometimes, they were right.

If there was one characteristic that helped me over the years, it was having a somewhat overactive sense of humor. We worked long hours under real pressure and some respite was needed. I particularly liked Halloween and usually wore costumes to work. Some of my colleagues did likewise. I once wore a gorilla costume into Bill Webster's morning staff meeting on Halloween and sat down in my usual place. I will give him credit. He did not say a word but continued going around the table and asking for the staff to report on their activities. When he came around to me, he said, "Dick, do you have anything to report?" I had decided early on that it was possible to do serious work without taking yourself too seriously.

I was not as erudite as some of my colleagues. My formal education was a bit limited and most of what I learned about writing and analysis had come from on-the-job training. Although I had some specific focus as a young analyst, I became a generalist without detailed knowledge of any particular country or issue. I often was too busy with the crisis of the day to focus on long range strategic planning. A bit more work on longer-term policy issues may have saved the CIA some future pain. Through the years, I made a number of mistakes in not pushing analysts or not knowing or asking the right questions. Some critics of intelligence believe that the CIA should know more than the participants in an unfolding crisis.

On balance, I believe that I was a positive force in helping produce some extraordinary analysis. The best way I can describe my role was as the frontman and spokesman for an able group of intelligence officers and analysts. I knew who were the most capable. I had a reasonably good command of the substance. I was not afraid of confrontation.

I believe that I understood the limitations and strengths of intelligence. As one of my colleagues said, there are two categories of uncertainty: secrets and mysteries. Many intelligence problems are in the category of mysteries because even the primary participants do not know what they will do or the implications of their decisions. There is no way to dig out the information if it does not exist. I had thought for some time that if we had access to Yeltsin's personal safe, we would not find any great secrets or plans for some evil deed. It is more likely that we might just find a partially consumed bottle of vodka.

The CIA has been criticized for a number of analytic failures. Some of these failures were because we had too little information, others because we sometimes ignored information that ran counter to our preconceived views. Intelligence probably makes its most useful contribution when it assesses the range of possible outcomes in a particular situation and then tries to describe the implications of these outcomes. A good example was the CIA analysis looking ahead at the Nicaraguan election in 1990. It concluded that the Sandinistas would win. Wrong! What it did well was to present the implications of victory by the Sandinistas or Chamorro. A key lesson is that the CIA is no better at predicting the outcome of elections than US media pundits and even the candidates themselves.

There are relatively few occasions when intelligence provides a flash of insight into a major national foreign policy issue. More often, intelligence analysis is a process involving the gradual accumulation of information and growing understanding. In some cases, its information trails behind that of the policymaker who often is in direct contact with the principal players. One word of caution: senior officials sometimes believe that their counterparts would never lie to them. The hard data on the military forces of potential adversaries is one thing intelligence provides in great detail and with considerable precision. The capability to provide information about intentions was often very limited. Nevertheless, there are numerous examples when calls by CIA and other intelligence organizations made a clear difference in the direction of policy. These range from the conclusion that the Soviets were withdrawing missiles and nuclear weapons from Cuba to the judgment that the coup against Gorbachev in August 1991 was not going to get off the ground.

The real value of intelligence is the day-to-day contribution to understanding the current set of problems and attention to problems that are just over the hill and not being considered by the policymakers. The continuity and experience of expert analysts working with managers who recognize good work when they see it is key. Great dramatic successes are only slightly less frequent than great dramatic failures, although you would never know it if your opinion was based on press coverage.

A Spy In Our Midst

During my tenure, there is one area where I wonder if I could have done better because it was a real disaster for the CIA and the nation—the Aldrich Ames espionage scandal. One clear responsibility of the agency was to collect clandestine intelligence by recruiting foreign agents. Part and parcel of that responsibility is the requirement to protect sources. In the Ames case, the CIA fell down on a core responsibility to ensure the trustworthiness of its officers and to protect its sources.

Bill Webster had been very aggressive in placing counterintelligence as a priority activity inside the CIA. He formed the Counterintelligence Center and insisted that it be manned by high-quality people. But that action came several years after Ames had already provided the information that doomed many of our sources inside the USSR.

I was first briefed on concerns about the security of

our overseas agents after I became the Deputy Director in 1989. A number of key Soviet sources had been rolled up by the KGB. It was unclear whether the compromises that had been identified were the result of technical problems, operational shortcomings, or a mole. The one thing certain was the damage done to our clandestine network and a significant loss of intelligence on the Soviet Union.

Although I continued to get bits and pieces of the continuing investigation, I never received another comprehensive briefing. My assumption was that the group trying to solve this problem was on top of it and would come back when it had additional information or needed guidance. It did not come back for either although there was no question in my mind that it was pursing the reason for the compromise as aggressively as possible. But I did not go to the group and push to get answers about what was going on. I would have done that on any major substantive problem of concern. Did they need more resources? Did they have administrative or bureaucratic blocks in their way? Appropriate questions that I should have asked.

I assumed others were closely following this problem. As the former head of the FBI and advocate of the new Counterintelligence Center, Bill Webster was much more expert in this area than I was. In fact, I did not know the people involved, and I had never worked on a major counterintelligence problem or paid much attention to this area of intelligence. I realize these are not adequate excuses, but those were my thoughts at the time. What are the facts? Who has been compromised? Who had access to the information? The questions are not all that different from those pertinent in other intelligence problems.

I should have focused on that issue, followed it closely, questioned those working on the case, and tried to identify what could be done to intensify the search. One of the difficulties for me and for others in the organization was that we were reluctant to believe that a CIA officer would betray the country and the organization.

Aldrich Ames was arrested in February 1994, a year after I retired from CIA. He had compromised many clandestine operations and probably caused a dozen key Soviets sources to be executed and many more imprisoned. He sold out the US for $4.5 million.

George Bush

One surprising outcome of my tenure has been my relationship with President George Herbert Walker Bush, with whom I became first acquainted during those briefings after the 1980 election. I assumed my contact with him ended with my retirement, although I did have a couple of debates during his election campaign against Clinton.

Years went by and my wife and I received an invitation to come to the Bush Library at College Station to celebrate the 25th anniversary of the Bush Administration. It was grand. A key part of the presentations was a mock meeting of the Deputies Committee chaired by Bob Gates and including most of the committee members. Jan and I met with President and Mrs. Bush in their library apartment, attended a grand dinner, and talked to the various members of the Bush cabinet in a very happy reunion.

I was again invited to the Bush library a couple of years later, this time to participate in a discussion in the library theater of a book just published describing the history of the President's Daily Brief. *The President's Book of Secrets* written by David Priess was a thorough review of the PDB history. I had talked in depth with the author and together with Carmen Medina, who had been a PDB briefer, joined the author in a presentation discussing the book. Jan and I once again got pictures taken with the President in the apartment.

In the Fall 2018, I received an e-mail from the Bush 41 staff alerting me that I (and one guest) would be invited to an upcoming celebration of Bush 41. The note did not say "funeral." Another note arrived shortly after his death, giving the schedule for the service to be held at the National Cathedral and instruction for guests. It was as carefully planned as the Normandy Invasion—go to a hotel, pick up ticket, go back the next day, go through security, board a bus and arrive at the cathedral three hours before the ceremony. I took my daughter and we went through the process and the wonderful ceremony—a celebration of a great life.

CIA in Decline

Even though I am no longer professionally associated with the Agency, over the past 10 years or so it's been unsettling to witness the decline of the CIA as a force in the national security apparatus of the US government. More and more emphasis has been placed on the Intelligence Community and particularly on the role of intelligence in supporting the US military. In the process of strengthening the "community," it appears the CIA has been diminished. It is no longer a "full service" organization with major responsibilities for collection, processing, analysis and reporting intelligence. Its primary role in the collection and analysis of imagery has been taken away and given to Defense. Its key role of providing direction in the development of technical programs was lost when the office that played this role was integrated into the National Reconnaissance Office (NRO). The CIA, and consequently the DCI, is now just one of many voices trying to get its priorities heard. It no longer dominates the technical development process nor determines collection priorities. The Defense Department is the dominant player in these activities.

There is no doubt that support to the military operators is a key mission. But in committing more and more resources to that effort, the agency has neglected some of its basic responsibilities for strategic intelligence to serve both civilian and military policymakers. The US Defense Department is very competent and proficient at providing policymakers options for using military force to address national security problems.

For nearly 30 years, I operated on the premise that the objective of intelligence was to provide to the policymaker the full range of information necessary develop policy options. I also believe that the use of military force was the most extreme option. Obviously, during the Cold War military action could have led to a direct confrontation. I continue to believe that the civilian departments and agencies should be brought into the process in a much more aggressive way. They should be in the position of offering a variety of options for action in the same competent way as the Defense Department. This is not a criticism of the military. To the contrary, they are dominant in the process because they are very good, and the civilian departments and agencies are less capable.

Unfortunately, comments by former DCI John Brennan, and Director of National Intelligence James Clapper have only further undermined the reputation of the CIA and the Intelligence Community.

President Trump appears to have little confidence in the major foreign policy elements of the government—intelligence, defense, and the foreign service. Decisions are made at the top without much input from government experts who may actually have something useful to add.

That situation must change, but that means that the foreign policy institutions need to regain the confidence of the executive. They need to demonstrate that they are capable and loyal. Confidence must be earned. But the President must foster the relationship. It is not a one-way street.

10.

LEAVING CIA

I have never been one of those people in government who was counting off the days until I could ease into a life of meandering in a garden and meeting friends at the diner for daily diatribes on the state of the world. I was the exact opposite. Retirement was not something I craved, and when the time came, I was not ready. I had not prepared a place to land, I was not financially well off after sending four children to college, and I was not emotionally ready to leave the best job in government.

For a few weeks I did nothing except mope. Then over the next year, I tried stay involved in world events and wanted to be considered an important player in the world of intelligence. I gave interviews to anyone who called, I went on the Charlie Rose program, spent hours with *FRONTLINE*, and even had an interview with Sacha Baron Cohen. I knew "Borat" did the fake interviews but thought it would be fun. I said at the beginning that if he got too crazy, I would end the session and pretty much did when he asked what kind of punishment should be given to suicide bombers. After a few months of this, I straightened out and decided that there was enough to do to make life interesting and it was not necessary to be "in charge."

I ended up following two different routes at the same time. I got involved in the private sector as a member of corporate boards and also worked on a wide variety of government panels and committees. In 1993, I was asked to become the President of the Security Affairs Support Association, a nonprofit group that brought industry and the leaders of intelligence together. I served as President for several years.

In addition to the private sector, I was asked to serve on advisory panels at the Los Alamos, Sandia, and Livermore laboratories. I also worked on some projects for DCI Gates and Tenet, as well as the President's Foreign Advisory Board. At the CIA, I worked with a group trying to develop games and exercises looking at future problems and a variety of different outcomes. The purpose was not to get the right answer but to understand the full range of possibilities. I stayed in contact with a number of active and retired people from the Agency.

Oversight

Since it was formed in 1949, CIA has been overseen by a variety of organizations in the administration and congress as well as the press. This is not surprising given that the Agency has significant independent contracting authorities, recruited spies overseas, and was involved in supporting insurgencies and governments fighting insurgencies. It needed oversight.

Administrative Oversight

There was some debate about whether or not President Truman should even create a central intelligence organization. If there was one the Secretary of Defense believed it should be in his Department. At first the new Central Intelligence Agency did not have the responsibility for covert action; it rested in State Department, but the Secretary of State quickly decided that conducting covert actions would conflict with State's foreign policy mission.

Between the 1950s and early 2000 there were over ten different committees of the national security council that "oversaw" CIA, primarily in the area of covert operations. Some members of the early committees were scientists or technical leaders who pushed collection programs such as the U-2, SR-71 and photographic and signal satellite systems.

In 1963, I briefed the President's Foreign Intelligence Committee on Soviet activity in Cuba. In 1964 I briefed the President's Foreign Intelligence Advisory Board (FPIAB) on a newly discovered Soviet ground effects vehicle. I remember being very impressed by members of the committee. They included Clark Clifford, Edward Land, James Killian, Howard Baker and General Jimmy Doolittle.

In the late 1990s, I was asked by the Chairman of the Board to give a "State of the Agency" talk to the full board. I do not have the text of that talk, but it emphasized the need for an independent and strong CIA with leadership drawn from the organization. I was bothered that several directors and their deputies had no direct experience with the Agency. How could they run an organization when they knew none of the key people and nothing of its culture? I also expressed concern that too much of the Agency's activities were in direct support of the DoD at the expense of other strategic problems.

Congressional Oversight

When CIA was established oversight in Congress was assigned to the Armed Services Committee and the Appropriations Defense Subcommittee. In fact, oversight was accomplished primarily between the DCI and the chairmen and ranking minority members of those committees. I mentioned an example of this when DCI McCone got approval for a major program after briefing the chairman of the Armed Service Committee.

Things changed in the late 1970s when after revelation of some serious errors in judgment by CIA, the Congress established the Senate Select Committee for Intelligence (SSCI) and the House Permanent Select Committee for Intelligence (HPSCI).

Many of the CIA activities that were publicized had been briefed to individual congressmen, but that did not keep them from acting totally surprise and outraged. There needed to be a process and a staff that kept track of what the Agency was up to. Like it or not, CIA was going to get oversight.

Personally, I have mixed views about the oversight process. On balance, I think it was a positive thing. Involving the Congress in the details of its activities gave the organization "some" protection when problems occurred. It also garnered support for many programs. The problem was that when confronted with a real issue involving intelligence activities, particularly covert action, the committees retreated, leaving the Agency out to dry.

Covert action often was the crux of oversight problems. Congress often did not agree with a foreign policy objective that CIA was trying to support. It was easier to attack the Agency than change the policy.

My involvement in congressional briefings falls into two categories. First, I was a bag carrier and vu-graph changer with a limited role unless asked by a Director to provide some specific facts. I helped the DCI's speechwriter, Pat Conger, prepare text although this talented former press correspondent was a master drafter. It was not until I became the Associate Director of Intelligence that I had a primary speaking role at Congressional briefings. As Deputy Director of Intelligence, I regularly went to the Hill, briefing both Senate and House committees. Over the years, as Associate Deputy and Deputy for Intelligence and as Deputy and Acting Director of CIA, I must have made over 100 appearances before Congress. Believe it or not, I actually enjoyed most of these briefings. I did think they were a positive in the relationship. I consider some of the staff chiefs to be personal friends although some on the staff liked to make trouble.

When I left the Agency, I received formal statements of appreciation in the Congressional record from Dave McCurdy and Bud Shuster, Committee Chairman. I particularly appreciated the format and consideration of Lee Hamilton when he was head of the HPSCI.

Another Briefing

In November 1995, I was asked to appear at the House Intelligence Committee. I had been vocal in my concerns about the Agency after retiring and was asked to share my thought on the Agency and the Intelligence Community.

In my presentation, I did not address all aspect of the problems facing the Agency but focused on the nation's need for a strong independent intelligence agency. I stressed the importance of strong leadership and the belief that the director should not be selected from the US military. Intelligence is a profession and either the director or deputy director should be a career intelligence officer. Putting people in these positions who have no knowledge of the culture or strengths and weaknesses of the Agency is a recipe for disaster. Military officers have many strengths but disagreeing with superiors probably is not one of them. CIA's special authorities and amazing program managers meant that large technical collection programs could be brought into operation quickly and without the endless bureaucratic wrangling. I cited the U-2, SR-71 and imagery and signals satellite programs as examples. It was important that CIA remain a leader in technical collection.

In the area of intelligence analysis, I was concerned that the focus was current intelligence and support to the US military. These are important areas, but longer-term analysis of developments in China, maintaining expertise about arms control, economic analysis and a host of other long-range issues are key to CIA's value.

One more experience with the Hill: Several years after my testimony before the committee a former senior HPSCI staffer asked me to sit in on a discussion with the head of the committee. He hoped we might help improve relations. We had a useful discussion although it was clear that the Chairman did not trust CIA. In fact, he insisted that the Agency regularly lied to the oversight committee. I found his comments striking.

I can honestly say I never lied to the oversight committees although there were times when I was not ready to raise a particular problem.

Press Oversight

I had a strict rule about not talking to the press unless directed to by a boss. When I retired, I changed my mind. I felt an obligation to defend the CIA from what became increasingly strong attacks. Also, as I have mentioned earlier some of CIA's important functions, technical intelligence programs and photographic interpretation, were being taken away from the organization. I was also concerned about CIA leadership. The next few directors and deputies that followed Bob Gates came from outside the CIA.

I began to express my concerns to those who would listen. I even accepted interviews with *Mother Jones* and similar publications. Perhaps the most significant and certainly the longest press interview I had was with *FRONTLINE*. That taped interview lasted for over two hours and covered a full range of topics including intelligence prior to the Iraq war, the issue of whether or not too much political pressure was placed on the Agency and interaction with Vice President Cheney. My comments on intelligence prior to the war with Iraq were identical to those expressed in other parts of this memoir. I told *FRONTLINE* interviewers that I thought Cheney's interaction with the Agency prior to the war was exactly what I would expect from an interested and demanding customer. He asked hard questions. I had many opportunities to deal face to face with the Cheney when he was Secretary of Defense and a member of Congress and found him to be thoughtful and always interested in intelligence.

CIA Inspector General

In addition to outside oversight the Agency has its own internal watchdog, the Inspector General (IG). In the late 1990s, the US Congress passed a law that the CIA IG would be confirmed by Congress and that it would regularly report on its activities to Congress. I disagreed with the law because it meant that responsibility for addressing grievances and illegal activities reported by CIA personnel would be taken out of the hand of CIA management and given to a congressional committee and staff.

Dr. James Schlesinger

James Schlesinger asked me to join the Board of Trustees of the MITRE Corporation a year or so after I began some consulting work with Mitre. When Schlesinger was Director of the Central Intelligence Agency, I saw him only once in the CIA barbershop. A steely-eyed character, an unsmiling face, getting a military-style haircut. I tried not to make eye contact. He spent less than a year at the CIA. Some would say his tenure was notable only for the number of people fired during the few months he occupied the position.

Twenty years later, I saw him a second time when he interviewed me for the position on the MITRE Board of Trustees. During the interview, Jim was interested in where in the Agency I had worked and what projects I had been involved in since retiring. He remarked on my serving on advisory boards for the National Laboratories at Los Alamos, Sandia, and Livermore. Having headed the Atomic Energy Commission and the Department of Energy, he remained interested in work at the labs, I found out later that there was very little that went on in the national security area that he was not interested in.

As Chairman of the MITRE Board, Jim's interests ranged widely. But he had a particular focus on intelligence projects and headed a committee that oversaw these activities. I was included on that committee together with John Hamre, Senator Chuck Robb, and three senior MITRE officers. Because MITRE's involvement in intelligence was extensive and complex, I had a good deal of personal contact with Jim from the beginning of my service on the board. He was particularly interested in my seven-year involvement with an international commission monitoring compliance with the Good Friday Agreement in Northern Ireland, and a review I headed that looked at intelligence provided to policymakers before the war with Iraq.

During my ten years on the MITRE Board of Trustees, there were many opportunities for conversations with Jim before and after meetings and during the regular dinners he hosted for principal customers, board members, and their spouses. Jim could be a pretty intimidating figure, and many walked around him with particular care. Some of the wives were a bit intimidated by Jim; my wife was not one of them. They became friends.

At each of the MITRE dinners held in Virginia or at the site of a major customer, Jim would deliver a short but sometimes politically incorrect talk. It was always amusing and always had a historic reference to some event that happened on the current date. Sometimes these talks were slow in coming as Jim engaged a guest in conversation. At one dinner, I got everyone at my table to begin running their fingers around the top of wine glasses and singing. The intent was to signal that it was time for Jim's talk. The idea caught on and from then on at each dinner there would be something happening at my table: the wave, Groucho Marx glasses and mustaches, and so on. Jim took all this with good humor although he would say, "The Kerr table is acting up again." I think he actually looked forward to the silliness.

During my terms as a Board member, Jim regularly tried to get me back into government. He set up appointments for interviews with White House staff searching for a head of TSA and a senior position at Homeland Security. I did not fit their model and was not particularly interested in the positions, but I did not tell Jim. In what may have been an attempt to round off some of my rough edges and put me in touch with the "right people," Jim also invited me to events such as the Gridiron Club dinner and the dinner of the Military Order of the Carabao. He included me in some groups reviewing arms control issues and made me a regular at a foreign policy round table he sponsored at Georgetown University. All in all, he tried to keep me engaged in Washington's business.

I continued to stay in contact with Jim after I left the MITRE board. I would call his office or visit him there, and after his health declined, at his home. We were very comfortable with one another and talked about our past, what was going on in the world, and what books or articles we were reading or should read. Unlike many who had rich experiences and served in positions of authority, he was not inclined to talk about the past as much as the present and future. Although he had a reputation for speaking his mind and being abrasive, he had a great sense of humor, and he was kind and thoughtful to others. Perhaps he had mellowed.

After Jim's death, I was both surprised and honored that he wanted me to be one of the four speakers at his memorial. I have many acquaintances and colleagues but few close friends. Dr. Schlesinger was one of those. At the ceremony I said Jim's death left a hole in my heart.

After MITRE, my service on boards continued. In 1998, I became an Outside Director for Marconi North America, and in 1999 joined the Board of Directors for Wang Government Services. All of these activities were great learning experiences. I believe my experience in the Intelligence Community was important training for working in the private sector. Although some of the financial issues were new, the basic problems of people and direction were very familiar. In hindsight, I believe working in the private sector for a period during my Agency career may have been very helpful experience.

I also worked with a group that reviewed the first briefing prepared in the Department of Energy describing the Chinese theft of US nuclear weapons secrets. Fortunately, the action plan developed by that group in 1997 looked very good, even in hindsight. Unfortunately, the group was disbanded. I subsequently served on a panel headed by Admiral David Jeremiah (Ret.) to assess the damage done to the US and the advantage gained by the PRC. Around this time, I was asked by the CEO of ManTech International to form a board of advisers for his company. I also joined the board of advisors of Aegis Research.

Watching from Afar

I did not have much direct contact with the Agency after I retired except for several studies for DCI Tenet. I followed foreign policy development and intelligence comments with keen interest. Once an analyst, always an analyst.

During the period of the Arab Spring, I followed events with particular interest only to find that it was primarily the State and Defense Department that provided public assessments of what was happening.

At one point I became very frustrated with US policy toward Libya, Syria, Egypt, and Iran and wrote a note to DCI Brennan expressing my concern. I put on a ragged CIA hat that had been through the laundry and sent him a note and picture indicating that I was concerned that CIA analysis was in tatters like my hat. I said that it appeared that either the Agency was not providing clear intelligence on the situation in the Middle East or the President was ignoring those assessments. He responded with a note reassuring me that all was well.

11.

RUSSIA AND BEYOND

Although I had been involved in following the Soviet Union since the early 1960s, I had never traveled to Russia. The CIA was not enthusiastic about having its personnel with sensitive clearances wandering around the world without very good reason.

A couple of years after I retired a friend and old colleague involved with a Washington think tank trying to improve US-Russian relations asked if I was interested in joining a delegation that was going to hold discussions in Moscow with some former Gorbachev associates, the moderates in Russia. It sounded like an interesting opportunity, and I signed up to go. Upon arrival, we were put up in one of the old government hotels that looked like something out of the Stalin era. I am sure if I had asked for a glass of vodka while standing alone in the center of my hotel room, someone would have knocked on the door with a bottle a moment later.

The meetings were interesting and lasted a couple of days with the focus on how we might improve and soften relations, which were pretty rocky at the time. One of my colleagues and I arranged a visit with the head of the KGB. The meeting was very perfunctory, and no issues of substance were raised. I decided it would be appropriate to wear my CIA tie to the meeting, and I called attention to it when the head of the KGB presented us with bottles of vodka.

We left the meeting and immediately drove out into the countryside. We were off to the birthday party of one of the leading Russian dissidents and a member of the Duma. I am not quite sure how we got invited, and I thought we were going to a large estate. In fact, we arrived at what looked like a hunting or fishing camp.

My friend and I were dressed in business suits; the rest of the guests and the host were in casual clothes. After several rounds of vodka and songs and more vodka, I pulled off my CIA tie and gave it to our host as a birthday present. He was immensely pleased and put it on with his plaid shirt and shorts. Although only a few of the dozens of guests spoke English, we managed to communicate rather well and in fact I was invited to attend the opening of a US muscle car company the next day by someone who spoke no English.

A few days later, the fellow I had given the tie to was killed on a street in downtown Moscow by an assassin riding a motorcycle. To my knowledge, no one was ever arrested for the crime. He was just one of several important critics of the government who were murdered during this period.

In the fall of 1998, I received a letter from Miroslav Tudman asking if I would join the editorial board of a new journal that would be published in Croatia. The journal would cover intelligence and policy issues in South and Eastern Europe. Miro Tudman was the former head of Croatian intelligence and the son the first President of Croatia. He was putting together a board comprised of the heads or deputies of western intelligence services and some academics. A friend of mine, Dick Stolz, the former head of the CIA clandestine service, also was invited to join.

All of us were asked to come to Dubrovnik with our wives in February 1999 to discuss the journal. The Stolzs and the Kerrs decided it was a wonderful opportunity and planned a trip that started in Venice, went to Trieste and then through Zagreb to Dubrovnik, the site of the conference.

After a couple of days in Venice, we took the train to Trieste located in Northern Italy on the Adriatic near the border with Slovenia. Trieste was the fourth-largest city in the Austro-Hungarian Empire after Vienna, Budapest, and Prague, and to this day is a major shipping center for Central Europe. Dick Stolz and his wife Betty had spent their first CIA assignment in Trieste in the first years of the Cold War and both were excited to return. Jan and I had never been to Trieste but were excited as well.

In an amusing coincidence, we stayed at a hotel in Trieste that had been the watering hole for Americans in the 1950s. At the hotel, the Stolzs met the manager who had been the busboy when they frequented the place fifty years earlier. He managed to find a photograph of all of them taken in those early days. It was a grand reunion with the appropriate toasts continuing into the night. The next day, we crossed the border into Slovenia to visit the training site for the famous Lipizzaner horses and a few sites where Dick had operated as a case officer.

Jan and I had been looking forward to the next stage of our journey—a night train trip from Trieste to Zagreb. It sounded like something out of an Agatha Christie novel. We boarded the train at midnight, finding our compartment. It was very depressing—iron metal bunks covered by brown army blankets. No wine, no music, no heat! We slept with our clothes on but only for an hour or so. The train suddenly came to a heaving halt, boots were heard in the companionway and there was a loud pounding on the compartment door. "Passports, passports!" demanded the border guard. She looked every bit like a border guard, carrying an automatic weapon and wearing an unfriendly face. I thought I had seen her before in a James Bond movie about East Germany. Dig out the passport and hope she does not arrest us.

Off again, we had made it through the Italian-Slovak border only a few miles from Trieste. What next? We needed to go to bathroom after that experience and made our way down the swaying corridor. Inside the smelly little room, we lifted up the toilet seat only to see railroad ties flashing by. The EPA would not like this sewage disposal system.

Putting our heads down on the dirty pillowcases, we dozed off only to once again hear the screech of brakes, the pounding on compartment door, and cries of "passport, passport!" This time it was the Slovenian-Croatian border officials carrying weapons and looking very formidable. They grabbed our passports but this time they took them into the corridor and spent a good deal of time deep in conversation while looking at our passports and talking into their radios. We were done for, two former Deputy Directors of CIA hauled off to prison in handcuffs. Had we told the Agency we were going on this trip? What will become of Jan and Betty? The border guards finally decided that we were harmless and let the four of us continue on to Zagreb.

We arrived in Zagreb at about 0500, tired and a bit disappointed in our less than glamorous train trip. Fortunately, Dick Stolz had been rather far sighted and made reservations for an early-morning check-in at a Zagreb hotel. We crashed and had a late breakfast before taking a taxi to the airport for our flight to Dubrovnik.

Dubrovnik is one of the beautiful cities, perched on the Dalmatian coast in the Adriatic. It is a grand, walled city and has been one of the great trading cities in the Mediterranean for centuries. During the war between Serbia and Croatia, it was regularly shelled from the high ridge overlooking the city. The population took refuge in a huge storage area under the main plaza. Dozens of houses inside the walls were destroyed.

Miro Tudman had brought together in Dubrovnik a wide variety of former heads or deputies of Western and Bloc intelligence services to serve as a board for a journal he was publishing. The group included the former deputy of the Bulgarian intelligence service, the former director of the Czech service, the former deputy director of the Soviet KGB, the former director of operations for the CIA and me, a former Deputy Director of CIA. In addition, the board included Dr. Agrell and Professor Dedijer, both of Lund University in Sweden, and Ambassador Medimorec from the Foreign Ministry in Zagreb. Marcus Wolf, the former head of East German Intelligence, and Admiral Lacoste, former director of French intelligence, also were invited to the conference but not as members of the board.

You might expect that this would be a very contentious group, with people on opposing sides during the Cold War. Clearer enemies could not be found—the CIA, French and Czechs on one side and the East German, KGB, and Bulgarians on the other. The strange thing was that this group had more in common with each other than it would have with its own citizenry. The group had very clear eyes about its jobs and objectives of their nations during the Cold War. Everyone spoke the same professional language even if it was in a different tongue. No one had to explain the nuances of intelligence collection or analysis or the difficulties of dealing with policymakers. They all understood the "business" of intelligence and its critical involvement in the foreign affairs of their countries.

The most controversial member of the group was Marcus Wolf, the former head of East German Intelligence, the Stasi. He was the only former head of an intelligence service to have been "defeated" in the Cold War and he was very bitter about his treatment in the new, unified Germany. He had forgotten that the victors write the histories. (There will be a bit more detail on him in the next piece describing a meeting in Bulgaria.) The East German service was abolished with much publicity, and it became the most memorable evil of the country. With the exception of Wolf, many of the retirees served in varying capacities as consultants to intelligence and policy agencies in their respective countries. They were not enemies in their own countries.

I had many long conversations with members of the group. In particular, I found the former Deputy Director of the KGB particularly interesting. He was a specialist in the Middle East and South Asia, and we had some long discussions about Afghanistan. He worked one side and I worked the other. At one point, we talked about how our customers reacted to the information we provide. We both used the word "customer" to describe those we worked for. In particular, we discussed what kind of reporting they had confidence in and when they were skeptical. He indicated that the Soviet leadership preferred documentary intelligence—reports and hard copy memorandum. I thought that my customers were more impressed by technical intelligence—signals, photographic, and technical analysis and had little patience with "expert" country analysis. Our experiences were quite similar and at one point I suggested that we co-author an article on the subject of the relations between CIA and its customers and the KGB and its customers. He considered the idea for some time but decided that he would be putting himself at risk.

The five wives spent their time sightseeing and taking breaks for lunch and tea. There was no common language, but a couple knew Italian, a couple German, and a couple French so it was possible to hold a roundabout conversation. Most conversations, however, involved only two people.

We had some wonderful dinners of fish and wild game served with great Croatian wine. The conversations were rich and in addition to Marcus Wolf, one person made a particular impression on me, Stevan Dedijer. He was an American citizen who had jumped into Normandy with the 101st Airborne, was a communist and once worked for CIA before he settled in Sweden. I kept in touch with him for several years, in part because it was interesting to exchange views with a real communist intellectual. It was fun to listen to his stories and still wonder about he was able to work at the CIA with such a strong bent toward Communism. But I believe many of his stories were true.

The conference was a great success considering the journal was published for several years and seemed to have a strong readership. Miro's interest in the journal waned a bit as he got more and more involved in Croatian politics. It was a worthwhile project and a fascinating trip.

In February of 1999, during the meeting of senior retired intelligence officers in Dubrovnik, the idea of a book containing the biographies of former chiefs and deputies of Western and former Bloc countries took shape. It was the brainchild of General Todor Boyadjjev, the former deputy of the Bulgarian intelligence service.

My first reaction was negative. I had retired from the CIA only six years earlier and was not sure that an autobiography was either appropriate or possible. But in the end, I was persuaded by my friend Dick Stolz, who had a fairly long association with Todor, my own ego, and the idea of leaving some memoir for my family. I completed the forty-page chapter and sent it to a CIA review board, and it was subsequently published in a book form in 2000. I should add that it was initially published in Bulgarian; an English version came out six years later.

The book contained ten chapters written by seven former intelligence officers, and three other pieces: one written George Tenet, the Director of Central Intelligence, two written by Kim Philby, a deceased British turncoat, and an article by Miro Tudman. The chapters are a mixed bag of commentary on intelligence and personal histories.

Most of the authors attended the book publishing event in Sofia in 2000. Sofia, the capital of Bulgaria, is an ancient city that predates the Roman Empire. As an honored guest, I was not given a suite in a relatively new hotel downtown and next to the area where the conference and book signing was held. No, I was put up in a historic house on a hill overlooking the city, a wooden house built in 1600's with ancient plumbing and a bed with rope strung under a thin mattress. The house creaked in the slightest wind, shutters and doors banged, and the place seemed alive. Several times during the night, I thought I heard people walking around in the house, although I knew I was the only occupant. The next morning, I walked down the hill to the city, passing a Roman coliseum where a group of actors were rehearsing.

The first event of the conference was a series of speakers talking about the "new" modern Bulgaria; one not under the yoke of Communism. A young man spoke about the evils of the previous regime and to my surprise, a group of middle-aged men in the audience, clearly former government apparatchiks, took off their shoes and begin pounding on the desks in front of them in protest. The young speaker did not miss a beat but continued to upbraid those unwilling to accept change. From that moment on when I attended speeches, I always thought about untying laces so I could quickly take off my shoes and pound on a table.

Most of the day involved speeches by those who contributed to the book. Perhaps the most memorable talk was given by Marcus Wolf. He clearly felt that the new unified Germany was treating him unjustly. In his speech he said the causes of the East and the West were equally justified, that he had just carried out the wishes of his country and was as much a patriot as other speakers. I followed him on the podium and said I just could not accept his view that the actions of both sides during the Cold War were morally equivalent. I said the East German government and its policies and treatment of its people were evil. People who implemented those policies could not escape the association and blame. I am afraid I put a cold blanket over the ceremony, and I did get a bit of the cold shoulder from Wolf and some of the Bulgarians for the rest of the conference. But life is short and then you die, and in between, you need to do what you think is right.

There was always a bit of uncertainty about who funded the conference and the book. I was introduced to Stephan, a "friend" of Todor who I decided must be the patron. Stephan had all the characteristics of the East European mafia. He was driven around in a black suburban with an armed driver and second man in the front and followed by a similar chase car. He also was accompanied by a beautiful and delightful "secretary" that could have been a former Miss East Europe. Stephan indicated that he was building a large resort on the Black Sea and invited my wife and me for a two-week visit. He would pay all expenses. He also offered to have his "secretary" and car take me on a tour of an ancient Orthodox Monastery located an hour out of Sofia. I decided that the trip to the Monastery would be interesting, but the trip to the Black Sea resort might be a bit over the top. I could see the headline in *The Washington Post:* "Former Head of CIA's Trip to Resort on Black Sea Paid for by Bulgarian Mafia."

The trip to the monastery was very worthwhile. It was

huge, with large living quarters for dozens of monks and beautifully built and decorated. It was built in the 1200's. We spent several hours touring the buildings and grounds which were heavily forested and crisscrossed by streams filled with live fish. After a delightful lunch and some excellent wine, the "secretary" and I made our way back to Sofia. Maybe I should reconsider a trip to the Black Sea resort.

Thrown into the War with Iraq

In the summer of 2001, I was involved in a project where a number of retired military and intelligence officers were brought into the CIA to assess work on Iraq. The group was given a series of briefings on Iraq, including the weapons program. After the session I was asked by a former commander of the Central Command what grade I would give to the intelligence presentations—I said a D. The next day, I happened to be invited to a "reunion" of former heads of the Intelligence Directorate. I told the head of the DDI that I was not impressed by the briefings we had received on Iraq and thought that the CIA's information and analysis on Iraq was pretty weak. She brushed off my comments with some offhand remarks, and I went on my way.

In the fall of 2001, it was obvious that the US was preparing for hostilities with Iraq. The Intelligence Community had been accumulating information that led them to conclude that Iraq was continuing an active program developing nuclear weapons. The war drums were beating in the Defense Department. Saddam Hussein did nothing to allay US fears.

Many in the Bush 41 Administration believed that a

preemptive attack on Iraq was unwise. I had mixed feelings. Getting rid of Saddam Hussein was certainly a positive step, but the idea of turning Iraq into some kind of democratic state seemed to be a bridge too far. How would we ever bring together the Shia, Sunni and Kurds into a cohesive government?

Later that year, Secretary of Defense Rumsfeld wrote a letter to George Tenet asking him to initiate a full assessment of the intelligence produced on Iraq. A second note from the Secretary a month later inquired about the status of this assessment, and the DCI somewhat belatedly decided to put together a study project. I was contacted and asked to form a team to review the intelligence produced over the previous year or so. I called three former senior intelligence officers who I knew were strong analysts with considerable experience in the subjects that we needed to address—the Middle East and specifically Iraq and weapons of mass destruction. They were Thomas H. Wolfe, who had served as Director of the Office of Near Eastern and South Asian Analysis, Rebecca L. Donegan who served as the Deputy Inspector General and in a variety of other positions, and Aris A. Pappas, an experienced military analyst.

The group, subsequently known as the Kerr Group, set up business in an office at the CIA headquarters and gathered together an extensive library of material that had been produced on Iraq and related issues over the past two years. The group had access to all the intelligence produced, including the most sensitive reports and communications to and from the White House.

The report focused on the intelligence process, product content, and analytic and collection shortcomings. It reviewed intelligence used to support judgments regarding weapons of mass destruction and to develop the National Intelligence Estimate on Iraq's weapons program. The product of the group was three separate reports two of them unclassified. The group did not interview analysts or managers but relied totally on the reporting it produced. We were concerned that if we began to talk with people, we would hear what they thought they reported or what they wanted to report rather than what actually went down on paper.

The reports concluded that analysis of the extent of Iraqi programs for developing weapons of mass destruction was clearly wide of the mark. It too often rested on old information acquired largely before late 1998 and was strongly influenced by untested, long-held assumptions. The analytic judgments rested almost solely on technical analysis, which has a natural tendency to put bits and pieces together as evidence of coherent programs and to equate programs to capabilities. As the result, the analysis, although understandable and explainable, arrived at conclusions that were seriously flawed, misleading and sometimes wrong.

In the spring of 2002, midway through the report, the Secretary of Defense asked for a status report on our progress. I scheduled a meeting with Secretary Rumsfeld that included George Tenet and Paul Wolfowitz. By that time, the group had a pretty good idea of the direction the report was going, and I offered a summary of the "bad news." Perhaps the most striking observation was my comment that it was clear that the Defense Department had not asked the CIA for any analysis of Iraq after the war and consequently had not received any information on what the Iraqi army might do when disarmed and dismissed. There was no request to the CIA for analysis of the reaction of the Muslim world to the "crusade-like" invasion of Iraq. The Secretary had no comment on my report.

Although the analysis of Iraqi WMD was flawed, a wide variety of intelligence produced on other issues involving Iraq was accurate. For example, topics such as how the war would develop and how Iraqi forces would or would not fight, as well as Iraq's links to al-Qaeda were well presented, as were calculations on impact of the war on oil markets.

The conclusions of the study disappointed me but the process of following the facts was one I learned during 30 years in the CIA. DCI Tenet never asked us to change our critical assessment of problems and shortcomings even though some of those judgments directly related to his performance. For example, the reports contained a number of observations about the problems of too close an association between intelligence and policy deliberations. We were concerned that the close and continuing personal contact between the DCI and policymakers probably imparted a greater sense of certainty to analytic conclusions than the facts would bear.

I had not completed the studies on Iraq when I became involved in another controversy, this one was hundreds of years old, the conflict in Northern Ireland.

PART III

BELFAST

Virgin Airlines was carrying me to London before another flight would take me to my final destination, Belfast. The Irish and British government had asked the US to provide a member to a four-man commission monitoring the peace treaty in Northern Ireland, the Good Friday Agreement. I had been contacted by the US Under Secretary of State to see if I was interested in the assignment. I accepted, thinking that it would be an interesting experience that would last for a year or so. In fact, it lasted for seven years. I was en route to meet the three other members of the Independent Monitoring Commission and develop the ground rules guiding our deliberations.

12.

THE "IRISH PROBLEM"

Richard Haass, the National Security Advisor under Secretary of State for Plans and Policy, called me in the summer of 2003 and asked if I was interested in serving on a four-man commission in Northern Ireland. The commission was to be set up by the United Kingdom and Ireland to monitor and report on paramilitary groups, "normalization" measures taken by the British government, and to consider claims that ran contrary to the agreement.

Haass and I served together in the Reagan and Bush Administrations. He was on the National Security Council staff. I was the Deputy Director of Central Intelligence and Central Intelligence Agency under George W. Bush. The idea of working on the conflict in Ireland was appealing. I accepted.

Little did I know the Independent Monitoring Commission (IMC) would continue for seven years, hold 107 meetings and present 26 reports. For me, that meant more than 400 days at airports and on aircraft flying to

Belfast and Dublin. For someone about to turn 70 in 2004, it was a strenuous routine.

The situation in Northern Ireland when the commission began its work was less violent than in the 1980s and 1990s. There were few attacks on security forces, but paramilitary groups were active, and violence was widespread. There had been 10 paramilitary murders the year before and shootings, extortion, and intimidation were common. The Northern Ireland Assembly was suspended in October 2003.

The IMC had four commissioners, two secretaries, and four other staff. The group was diverse: a former Northern Ireland politician and psychiatrist, a former senior Irish civil servant, a former senior British police officer, and a former deputy CIA director.

The commission first met in October 2003. We looked for examples of similar bodies and found none. We decided there would be no chairman. We also decided to be proactive and to influence the behavior of paramilitary groups, not just report on them. We saw our job as helping end the intimidation, violence, and criminality of paramilitary organizations, and helping the people of Northern Ireland live normal lives.

The commission attracted considerable attention ranging from extremely critical to enthusiastically supportive. One article referred to it as "three spooks and a Lord," noting the connection three commissioners had with intelligence and police, and the fact the Northern Ireland commissioner was in the House of Lords. Some in the press thought we were house pets of the Northern Ireland Police Service and British intelligence. But the commission established a positive reputation.

Just before the final report, an Irish Times editorial said the commission by "its regular comments on the continuing threat posed by loyalist and dissident republicans...has motivated politicians to reach difficult compromises rather than permit a slide back into anarchy."

The commission reported on more than 21 murders, 800 paramilitary casualties, the robbery of the Northern Bank, and a feud between the Ulster Volunteer Force and the Loyalist Volunteer Forces in which the UV murdered five people and the resurgence of violence by dissident republicans in 2009 and 2010. The commission also reported on robberies, kidnappings, smuggling, and other paramilitary criminal activities.

In addition to regular contact with the law enforcement and other agencies of the UK and Ireland, the commission met with political parties, community groups, churches, charities, pressure groups, former combatants, businesspeople, lawyers, journalists, academicians, victims, and private citizens.

There were positive developments during this period; most important was the commitment of the Provisional Irish Republican army to pursue peaceful means for change. Actions by loyalist paramilitaries to end their military campaign and decommission their weapons also were significant.

It is difficult to assess the commission's impact on the peace process. But the commissioners believed its reporting on the association between PIRA and Sinn Féin influenced the decision that the political path could no longer be pursued if there was a direct connection between the two organizations.

The commission held the leadership of these paramilitary organizations responsible for the crimes their organization committed but also gave them credit when their behavior changed. Perhaps its greatest achievement was to give the political parties confidence they could enter into a joint government.

Without the commission reports, it would have been difficult to get the Northern Irish Assembly and the executive restored in 2007 or to allow the policing and justice system to be returned to the Assembly's authority in 2010.

Clearly there were some lessons to be learned from the experience of the commission. The four commissioners brought different perspectives to the process. They followed the facts and continually questioned conclusions and tested confidence in the available material. The commission was particularly careful in wording its reports. It worked as a team while debating issues and the validity of information. The group spent an enormous amount of time reviewing reports, trying to get "it right."

The team's continuity was important. Regular meetings and a report format emphasized trends and facts. Keeping pressure on and returning to key issues meant that problems were not left behind just because we addressed them once.

The IMC was full of rich experiences. I talked with murderers in prison and rode around in communities with people who were convicted of murder and other crimes. I sat with victims and their families and listened to stories about the murders of children, brothers, and fathers, and the mutilation of young men shot through the knees because they crossed paramilitary bullies.

The cost of the violence in Northern Ireland was enormous and the toll was heavy. Nearly every citizen had a family member fall victim. Over the commission's seven years, violence declined significantly.

The team frequently disagreed about the importance of some information or the implications of a dramatic development. But it always softened disagreement with humor. We also had a book club. I had several T-shirts made for the group. One had a logo "Three Spooks and a Lord." Another a quote from P. J. O'Rourke "Always read something that will make you look good if you die in the middle of it."

I also realized Americans and Europeans thought about things differently. I was more inclined to be blunt with the people, sometimes making other commissioners uncomfortable. They were more careful in their language and in their drafting. They were more politically correct. I wanted to name the names of the leaders and criminals; they were worried (probably with some merit) about the legality of that. I thought we gave unwarranted respectability to terrorists, murderers, and criminals by referring to them as "paramilitaries."

One last discussion among the commissioners says it all. The other three commissioners were worried that our immunity to being hauled into court would end when the commission ended. We could end up in court if we subsequently said something that could be considered libelous or a violation of human rights or presented some contested piece of information. I realized that I was protected by the US Constitution and the right of freedom of speech. Neither Ireland nor the UK have such guarantees.

The governments of Ireland and the UK formally ended IMC activities in March of 2011. They offered a somewhat perfunctory "thank you" to the group after deciding that the normal law enforcement agencies could deal with the small dissident groups that continued their violent ways. Governments do not necessarily embrace oversight organizations that they do not control. In comments on the final report of the IMC in the House of Lords, Baroness Harris of Richmond congratulated the IMC on "their work, bravery, dedication and commitment to building of the very different Northern Ireland that we see today." I always wanted to be called "brave" by a baroness.

In 2012, I had been a member of the BAC Inc board for a number of years, serving as the head of the committee that ensured that the company followed the rules of a foreign-owned company involved in classified US government contracts. BAC was one of the sponsors of the Woodrow Wilson Foundation dinner giving Mrs. Clinton its annual award for public service. I was asked to represent the company at the dinner and ended up seated right next to her.

I was not a fan of Mrs. Clinton's politics but intended to be on my best behavior as a representative of a company sponsoring the event. The dinner was a grand gala attended by senior Democrat party members, friends of Mrs. Clinton and female supporters. Before dinner, I asked Mrs. Clinton about US policy toward Syria which was a hot topic and one that I was very interested in. We had a long and interesting conversation. I was quite critical of US policy and asked about Senator Kerry's dinner with Asad and his suggestion that there was reason for optimism about Syrian domestic policy. She defended US policy as expected. It was a good exchange, and the next day one of my fellow board members mentioned that it appeared that the two of us were talking to the exclusion of everyone else at the table.

In early October 2013, *Newsweek* organized a war game that simulated a mock attack by Israel on Iran's nuclear facilities. The "game" was run in a conference room at the Brookings Institution in Washington DC and the results were published a week later.

In the game scenario, Israeli aircraft heavily damaged Iranian nuclear facilities but the full extent of damage was unknown. Clearly, the attack would have set back the Iranian nuclear problem. It would not have ended that program. The attack was conducted without prior consultation with the US.

Newsweek asked seven former senior political, military, and intelligence officials to convene a "mock" meeting playing the roles of key presidential advisers—chief of staff, national security adviser, secretaries of state and defense, directors of national intelligence and the CIA and chairman of the Joint Chiefs of Staff. I was asked to act as the Director of National Intelligence, a role I relished.

The meeting followed the pattern used by most administrations to address crises. The issues discussed were surprisingly familiar to most of the participants—what were the facts on the ground, what response could be expected from the Iran, what was the likely regional and world reactions, and exactly how should the US respond?

Following the usual format, I was asked as the head of

intelligence to describe the situation on the ground but more particularly to outline things that the group needed to address. Based on my experience in these situations and some familiarity with the Middle East, I thought it likely Iran would continue firing missiles at Israel and would consider attacking US targets in the Middle East, but they would try to operate through proxies and keep their fingerprints off actions against the US. Cyber-attacks against the US, terrorist attacks against US facilities, and operations against US forces along the Iranian/Afghan border were likely, but the Iranians would avoid direct military confrontation with US forces. Some attacks on tankers in the Gulf were likely, but not attacks on US naval combatants. My intelligence partner at the session suggested that the Iranians would try to get Arab protesters into the streets and that we needed to at least consider that the Iranians might launch missiles armed with chemical weapons at Israel causing a major escalation of the war.

There was consensus among the policy making members of the group that a major objective of the US was to scale back tensions without signaling weakness to Iran, put some distance between the Israeli decision without walking away from Israel, and protect US citizens. The "Chairman of the Joint Chiefs" made it clear that the military was going to put itself in the position of defending itself and that meant be in the position of conducting "operational offense," not just defense. There was agreement that while the team urged de-escalation, an attack on American targets would inevitably lead the US to war. The policy group also came down strong in support for Israel and its security despite considerable angst over the fact that no advance warning had been provided, which put US personnel and interests in the area at risk.

There was considerable concern expressed that while the Israeli assault would set back the weapons program, it also would undermine US and international efforts to keep Iran from developing nuclear weapons. Tehran would withdraw from the Nuclear Proliferation Treaty, expel international observers, and the attack would lead to an unraveling of sanctions.

The group was well aware of the political implication of an Israeli attack on Iran the month before a national election. There was recognition that there would be no recommendations that were politically impossible. Consequently, there was no discussion of using the Israeli attack as an excuse for a massive US military effort to destroy Iranian nuclear facilities and perhaps work toward regime change.

The "game" showed how US interests and policy can be put at risk by the actions of others. Although the "game" only covered the first hours of the crisis, a policy framework was developed. Subsequent events would have stressed and altered the initial policy recommendations. Perhaps the major takeaway from the "game" was that there is a certain constancy to the intelligence and policy process. Even though I had not participated in a real meeting of the type described above for about 20 years, little had changed in the how problems are addressed, and policy developed.

As an aside, some of the participants told the reporter that "in real-life meetings, intelligence analysts might not allow themselves to be so opinionated." An interesting observation because in the many meetings on crises I attended, I was never bashful about expressing my opinion. Nearly any policy issue can be turned into an appropriate intelligence question.

Recent events in Benghazi, Libya, indicate that the process of moving decisions back to Washington for resolution in a thoughtful and careful manner may not allow for a quick and appropriate response. But the alternative is to give civilian and military personnel in the field the ability to make decisions that could have serious impact, setting in motion events that could spiral out of control. An interesting dilemma.

13.

LIFE ON THE WATER

Jan and I left Virginia a couple of years after retiring. We decided that if we stayed in the area, I would be over committed with work. Our youngest son, Kevin, was a builder on the Outer Banks of North Carolina. He was starting a family there and building houses. We decided to go down and look at property and build there. Although we originally intended to build a house near the sound, we were visiting friends who had rented a house on the ocean. As we were sitting out on deck overlooking the ocean that evening, we decided that was where we wanted to live. The next day, we began looking for houses and found an old house in a great location. We bought the house before we sold our house in Virginia, an unwise idea normally, but it worked out well and we ended up with Kevin tearing down most of the house and building a great house where we lived for more than a dozen years.

In 2010, after Kevin and his family moved to Hawaii, we began to feel a bit lonesome for children. Our daughter, Meagan, was pregnant and then a little boy, Quinn, was born. Jan and I decided that living near that new grandson would be ideal. We had a little townhouse in Vero Beach not far from Meagan and began looking for something more permanent. We found a house that had been vacant for two years. It was a large house surrounded by huge oak trees with a small guest cottage. A bit too fancy for us, but we were able to sell our house on the Outer Banks and had enough money to pay for the new house. Since it was just after the recession, we sold our house in the Outer Banks at its most depressed price but bought in Vero Beach under the same circumstance. Buy high and sell low.

Long hours and long weeks put a fair amount of pressure on the family, so Janice and the four children offered a real refuge from the day-to-day pressures. The family was close and remains so. The children all went off in their own direction. None was attracted to work on national security issues. Perhaps I talked too much about these issues and turned them off.

My wife was a major asset my entire career. She managed the family and the household. She took care of the books and was always there when the children came home from school. She had a number of different jobs that fit in with the schedule of children, including acting as an instructor for CIA officers going overseas, training them to detect surveillance. She was not particularly impressed by people of rank and high position and made sure I did not get too full of myself.

It was only recently that I realized how often I left Jan to take care of family, home, and miscellaneous crises while I wandered off. This began early, as I had only one week of leave when we got married and I was off for a month of training and reassignment with the US Army. I left her in a transitional neighborhood in Phoebus without friends, 3,000 miles away from relatives, and with a new baby while I went on a month-long exercise over Thanksgiving in Louisiana.

I worked long hours as a young analyst and even longer hours as a senior manager, often traveling overseas while leaving Jan behind to take care of three boys and a girl. While in Hawaii I decided that a tour in Laos would be more interesting than the job I had and left Jan with the boys and a daughter. Even after retiring, I spent considerable time away from the Outer Banks working in DC on various projects and then working for seven years on the Independent Monitoring Commission, spending three of four days a month in Ireland. I spent several days a month in DC for a period of twenty-odd years. Jan never complained about my absences. In fact, there were times when I began to be too much of a pest and Jan would say, "Don't you have anywhere to go?"

At one cocktail party in the residence of an ambassador, she was walking around a crowded room looking for someone who spoke English. She heard a man waxing on about something and went up and stood next to him. When he finished, she asked where he worked in government. The man said he was the Attorney General of the United States. She responded by saying that must be an interesting job. She walked away. At dinner, she was seated to his left.

At a dinner in the White House, she was placed next to a Mr. Gillespie at the head table. Always interested in people, she asked him what he did. He said he was a musician. Then she asked if he had recorded any albums.

He said that the albums would reach nearly to the ceiling. She then asked, "Do you have a nickname?" He said he did. "Would it be 'Dizzy?'" she asked.

Jan was a major asset on foreign trips. Her presence forced the hosts to bring their wives to social functions. That changed the nature of the gathering and often the conversations were much more interesting. In addition, she spent considerable time talking to Agency officers and secretaries and found out far more about their problems and concerns that I could in discussions with their bosses.

I am very proud of my three sons and daughter. They are people with all the right values. My oldest son, Randall, went to the University of Virginia, where he was a soccer star. He ended up in a successful property management business. My middle son, Andre, is an artist who most recently has been involved in building sets for movies. My youngest son, Kevin, is a builder and built our house on the Outer Banks of North Carolina. My daughter helps manage a plumbing company but is a closet farmer. Classy people! I love them all and perhaps more important I *like* them. They also have produced nine grandchildren with an age span of thirty years. The grandchildren keep me young and give me a place to spend money. We've had some great Christmas gatherings with my three children and nine grandchildren. Jan and I will have been married 70 years in 2022.

***

I have neglected mentioning my siblings and need to correct that. My brother, Claude, was five years older and our paths seldom crossed growing up. We remained in contact over the years and I got to know his two sons, Grant and Scott. He was a good person, a reborn Christian who practiced what he preached as a missionary.

My half-sister was ten years younger, and I lived with her only during three years of high school. She had MS as a young person and lived a largely unhappy life.

My half-brother Steve Heddy is ten years younger and lived with my stepfather after my mother died. He had an unusual upbringing but survived and now has a great wife and family. When we get together, we talk about our rather strange childhoods.

PART IV

VERO BEACH

Our travel from the Outer Banks of North Carolina to Vero Beach, Florida, was not by air. Getting away from storms and cold to live near my daughter, new grandson and my oldest son was a journey, nevertheless. In my adopted community, I found opportunities to speak to local groups and write foreign policy articles for a weekly magazine. I was asked to join a writer's group—the Sandfly Scribblers—just down from my house on Sandfly Lane, got involved with a group trying to organize an archeological dig at an Ice Age Site, and continued to serve on a couple of private sector boards in Washington DC. I even joined several others for a weekly talk show and published a book of short stories, *The Dark Side of Paradise,* in 2019. However, my interactions with the CIA did not come to an end.

14.

DIGGING VERO BEACH

Shortly after moving to Vero Beach, I heard about a group trying to organize a dig at an Ice Age site in the city. I had always been interested in archeology although not as far back in history as the Ice Age. I got involved with the group as it tried to raise funds locally, and with the state to re-excavate a site along a canal where the remains of dozens of Ice Age animals and several humans were found in early 1900.

One thing led to another and before I knew it, I was the vice chairman of the group. I got involved in getting Mercyhurst University to lead the venture and hiring a Florida archaeologist as the site leader of a project that started more than 100 years ago.

In 1914, a project began in Vero Beach to dig a canal as part of a drainage system that would keep much of the area from being a marshland. During the project, the crew came upon a surprising discovery, bones of Ice Age mammals and human remains. Dr. Elias Sellards, a Florida State geologist at the time, knew about Vero and the bones being found there. What got his attention were the human bones.

At the peak of the last Ice Age 20,000 years ago, a two-mile-high glacier covered the continent a thousand miles to the north. A Vero wetland existed that attracted the Ice Age mega-fauna—mammoths, mastodons, saber-toothed cats, huge sloths, and giant armadillos that roamed the land.

In 1916, Sellards came to Vero and found the remains of another human. This became known as the Vero Man. In addition, Sellards uncovered the bones of 23 types of extinct Ice Age mammals. Finding human remains in the same soil level in association with these mammals, he concluded that humans were there together during the Ice Age.

The Smithsonian's Dr. Aless Hrdlička declared Sellards wrong. The human remains were not Ice Age but Indian burials. The importance of Vero quickly diminished. An archaeologist at the Smithsonian inspected the skull of the Vero Man and declared it a woman.

In 2006, the City of Vero Beach planned a water treatment plant along the main canal. It required an archaeological review. In the meantime, James Kennedy found a bone with an etching of a mammoth on it. A scientific evaluation concluded that it was probably real.

A group of local citizens in 2010 formed the Old Vero Ice Age Site Committee (OVIASC) to re-investigate the site. OVIASC hired Dr. Andy Hemmings, an archaeologist with Florida experience who brought in Dr. James Adovasio of Mercyhurst University to direct an excavation that began in January 2014. The university worked the dig on a cost-shared basis with OVIASC. After removing eight feet of overburden by the canal to get to the 1916 surface, a weather port was put in place. Within that area, a crew of ten recent archaeology graduates began the meticulous excavation.

After the 2015 dig, Mercyhurst determined it could no longer afford to participate. OVIASC applied to the State of Florida and received grants over four years totaling $900,000. With matching funds from local donations and in-kind volunteer labor the excavation continued. Florida Atlantic University's Harbor Branch organization administered the grants and provided housing for the dig crew. Harbor Branch and Indian River State College performed DNA studies.

Nine geological soil levels going back 30,000 years were identified. The first indication of a human presence was stone flakes resulting from the sharpening of tools. Humans brought the stone to Vero from more than a hundred miles away. Pieces of charcoal indicated a possible fire pit. Bone fragments from extinct mammals were found. An 8,000-year-old piece of woven material was uncovered. At the end of the 2016 dig, a bison bone bed appeared. Near it were bones of an extinct tapir and the tip of a man-made bone needle. Post-Ice Age projectile points were found. Volunteers made many similar finds in the overburden dug from the excavation, but the items had no context in those disturbed soils.

The dig was completed in May of 2017. Almost 2,000 people toured the site that year. Analyses of the findings continued into 2018. More than 100 radiocarbon dates were obtained. DNA data proved difficult to determine due to the tropical nature of the site.

At an archaeological conference in 2018, Dr. Adovasio

reported that the intent had not been to validate Sellards' Ice Age human presence. The tapir with a bone-needle point was an indication, but not proof, of an Ice Age presence. But there was no doubt that people had been on the site 6,000 to 8,000 years ago. The projectile points of that period were an indication. A piece of textile weave found was similar to the material skeletons were buried in at another Florida site of that age. Vero was "apparently" a burial site.

With no absolute proof that Ice Age humans inhabited the Old Vero Site itself, they had been in the Vero area. A 12,000-year-old Clovis projectile point was found on a farm three miles away.

It was a great experience following the very sophisticated digs that occurred after 2014. I helped the committee change the sponsor of the dig from Mercyhurst to Florida Atlantic University and worked to get state funds to support future digs. While evidence of human presence was confirmed at the site, no significant artifacts have been uncovered.

It was an interesting, although somewhat frustrating, venture. The spot chosen for the excavation was an area of only about 3,000 feet. It was like looking for a needle in a haystack, which sometimes reminded me of various projects in my professional career.

15.

EPILOGUE – RESTORING THE IMPORTANCE OF THE INTELLIGENCE COMMUNITY

After 33 years working for the Central Intelligence Agency and another 20-some odd years as a consultant dealing with national security affairs, it is difficult to end this book without addressing the state of world affairs and the CIA.

As mentioned earlier, I am not a strategic thinker and was most effective writing about and managing crises and international problems of the day. Today, the world is an exciting place for an intelligence officer. Conflicts in the Middle East, Russian meddling, and negotiations with North Korea are not new but remain incredibly challenging. China has replaced the Soviet Union as the major threat, but from the perspective of an intelligence officer it represents an engrossing target.

Will China's aggressive efforts to control its population and become an economic and military peer of the US be upset by unrest in Hong Kong and Taiwan? Is Europe's attempt to bring about economic and political unity stumbling as it faces the appeals of nationalism? How will the world adapt to the movement of large numbers of displaced people who strain political and economic stability?

While the fear of international communism is gone, there is real and justifiable concern about the future of "democracies." Are the Chinese or some other model, a blend of economic freedom and near totalitarian political control, the future? These are questions that must be addressed by the Central Intelligence Agency.

The organization is not the same one I grew up in, for better or worse. The offices that "invented" satellite reconnaissance and photographic interpretation have been transferred to the Defense Department, and it is now a user, not a creator, of photographic intelligence. When it reorganized its analytic groups along geographic lines and eliminated its functional offices—economic, military, and scientific—it gradually focused on current intelligence at the expense of serious research. Collection and analysis aimed at the terrorist target and in support of US military operations weakened its in-depth understanding of key issues. The creation of the Director of National Intelligence (DNI) was a serious mistake made in the heated aftermath of the 9/11 crisis. The DNI eroded the strength of the Director of CIA, had little real authority, no troops, and added another bureaucratic layer.

The Central Intelligence Agency got off to a bad start with the Trump Administration. Statements by the former senior leaders of US intelligence pitted the organization against the President. The subsequent surfacing of a whistleblower during the impeachment inquiry furthered tensions. Encouraging CIA employees to publicly vent their disagreements with the administration is a path to the destruction of the Agency.

Despite its problems, the CIA remains a major asset of this and any administration. Analysts and operations officers must leave their political views at home. During the Cold War, the CIA built an impressive capability to assess military, economic, and social issues inside the Soviet Union. A similar capability assessing China is needed today and no organization other than the CIA is capable of such a challenge.

16.

PHOTOS

All photos courtesy of author's personal collection unless otherwise indicated.

Mr. and Mrs. Richard J. Kerr, newlyweds at Fort Ord in 1953

William Casey and Richard J. Kerr

An August 1987 National Security Meeting in the
White House
(Official White House Photo)

Richard Kerr wishes DCI William Webster well at his retirement

DDCI and head of Chinese military intelligence arguing over who was responsible for the disorder in Tiananmen Square

Kerr at one of the daily briefings with President Bush, September 1991
(Official White House Photo)

Kerr being sworn in as DDCI with Webster, President Bush, Justice Berger, and Jan Kerr

Independent Monitoring Commission – Richard Kerr, John Grieve, Irish Prime Minister, Lord John Alderdice, Joe Brosnin

George Patrick (Kerr's driver), Joy Starr, and Nickolas Starr who was badly wounded by a terrorist in front of CIA headquarters

Sue Shiff, part of Kerr's team and affectionately dubbed his "day wife"

Richard and Sue surrounded by coworkers at lunch on the CIA balcony

Kerr, others from CIA, and Afghan fighters gather on a Soviet tank

Retirement Party with Dick Helms, Ray Cline

Bob Gates, Jan Kerr

Kerr surrounded by two of his many costumes over the years

Mentors and friends from the CIA—Bruce C. Clarke Jr., John McMahon, John J. Hicks—and post-CIA Dr. James Schlesinger

The Agency says goodbye

Richard and Jan in front of the CIA Wall of Honor

Richard Kerr's children – Andre, Meagan, Kevin, Randy

The extended Kerr family

1948 Oldsmobile decorated for the Kerrs' 50th wedding anniversary

www.ingramcontent.com/pod-product-compliance
Lightning Source LLC
Chambersburg PA
CBHW062037120526
44592CB00035B/1204